T0248431

DIGITAL
CUSTOMER SUCCESS

FOREWORD BY
CHRISTINA KOSMOWSKI,
CEO, LOGICMONITOR ᴀɴᴅ FORMER CCO, SLACK

DIGITAL
CUSTOMER SUCCESS

WHY THE **NEXT FRONTIER** OF **CS** IS
DIGITAL AND **HOW YOU** CAN **LEVERAGE**
IT TO **DRIVE DURABLE GROWTH**

NICK
MEHTA

KELLIE
CAPOTE

Published by John Wiley & Sons, Inc., Hoboken, New Jersey.
Published simultaneously in Canada.

For general information on our other products and services or for technical support, please contact our Customer Care Department within the United States at (800) 762–2974, outside the United States at (317) 572–3993 or fax (317) 572–4002.

Wiley also publishes its books in a variety of electronic formats. Some content that appears in print may not be available in electronic formats. For more information about Wiley products, visit our web site at www.wiley.com.

Library of Congress Cataloging-in-Publication Data is Available:

ISBN: 9781394205875 (cloth)
ISBN: 9781394205882 (ePub)
ISBN: 9781394205899 (ePDF)

Cover Design and Image: Mohamed Mubasil Kamal Musthafa/Gainsight

SKY10069780_031524

Contents

Foreword   *vii*

Chapter 1   The High-Speed Evolution of Customer Success   1

Chapter 2   Durable Business Strategies to Fuel
Long-Term Success   19

Chapter 3   Digital Customer Success Is a Strategic Program   35

Chapter 4   The Digital Customer Success Maturity Model   53

Chapter 5   Launching the Proactive Phase of
Your Digital CS Program   71

Chapter 6   Evolving to the Personalized Phase   93

Chapter 7   Evolving to the Predictive Phase   111

Chapter 8   Launching Your First Digital Initiative   129

Chapter 9   Company-Wide Digital Program Governance
and Cross-Functional Collaboration   155

Chapter 10   Optimizing Your Digital Toolkit   175

Chapter 11   The Ability to Be More Human   197

Acknowledgments   *205*
About the Authors   *207*
Notes   *209*
Index   *215*

Foreword

By Christina Kosmowski, CEO, LogicMonitor

In the ever-evolving landscape of SaaS, I've had a firsthand view of the transformative power of Customer Success. I believe *Digital Customer Success* captures the essence of this journey, resonating with the very core of my professional career leading Customer Success teams at Salesforce, Slack, and now as CEO at LogicMonitor.

The digital era we're navigating is not just about technology; it's about people. It's about how we, as leaders, harness digital tools to amplify human connections and drive meaningful business outcomes. With this book, Nick Mehta and Kellie Capote dive into that very intersection, highlighting how businesses can thrive by prioritizing Customer Success at the core of a scalable, digital customer experience.

Throughout my career from CSM to CEO, I've learned that the key to sustainable growth lies in understanding and adapting to customer needs. This book echoes that sentiment and offers insights and strategies for anyone looking to excel in today's customer-driven business landscape.

What I find most compelling about this book is its pragmatic approach to digital Customer Success. It's a practical guide drawn from the real-world experiences of other CS practitioners. I've faced many of the challenges these authors and thought leaders from the Customer Success community have encountered, and through their lessons learned, readers will get a blueprint not only to navigate but also to lead in the digital age.

As you turn these pages, you'll discover why placing Customer Success at the heart of your growth strategy isn't just good practice; it's a business imperative. The book will equip you with the tools and knowledge to transform your organization, ensuring that your journey in Customer Success is as impactful and rewarding as mine has been.

Whether you're a budding CSM or a seasoned CEO, these pages hold the key to unlocking the full potential of your business and your career in Customer Success. My path has been shaped by the relentless pursuit of customer-centric innovation, and this book offers the roadmap for others to do the same.

1 | The High-Speed Evolution of Customer Success

It's a Friday night, and you've just arrived at your favorite corner bistro. Inside, the host warmly greets you by name before escorting you to a choice table. There, a familiar waiter smiles just before you suggest (as always) that there's no need to recite the specials. You'll have your usual entrée paired with a glass of your favorite varietal.

Now, *this* is what makes life worth living. It's not merely the food, though the food is spectacular. It's not merely the atmosphere and the view from your favorite table. No, what really keeps you coming back week after week, year after year, is the *personal* service, delivered by people who seem to genuinely care that *you* are having a wonderful experience.

In an increasingly impersonal world, a world where artificial intelligence (AI) informs you that "people who bought the pinot noir also purchased camembert and water crackers" and where "talking" with a customer service agent means interacting with a chatbot decision tree, who can blame you for craving a personalized experience—for wanting to go "where everybody knows your name and they're always glad you came"? Given a choice, wouldn't all of us prefer to be treated like unique individuals instead of data sets?

At Gainsight, our purpose statement is "to be living proof you can win in business while being Human-First." It's so easy to forget that the person on the other side of the video meeting isn't just a candidate, employee, alumni, prospect, customer, or investor—they are a human being first. We need to always remember that. But this raises a seemingly intractable question for every company in the software-as-a-service (SaaS) sector and beyond: How do you *scale* a Human-First customer experience?

Your favorite restaurant provides personalized service because the staff works at a single location every night, serving a small number of regular customers. In the beginning, the same is true of almost every tech start-up. Many founders talk to each of their early customers themselves. I remember one well-known founder who said, "I bring my laptop to the customer, watch them work, and code what they want." But once the owner of the restaurant or the start-up needs to scale, personalized experiences are often jettisoned in favor of a more efficient—and more impersonal—experience.

As business leaders, we recognize that we must scale up to build our companies, and the way to do this is through automated systems and processes. But must we also lose the human touch? Can't we find ways to efficiently scale without treating our customers like fungible cogs? Can we find ways to *enhance* the customer experience via automation?

The Human vs. Digital Dilemma

In the case of the restaurant, the answer is a qualified *yes*. Although most of us would not want to visit a restaurant in which we had to interact with robot waiters instead of humans, many of us would love to book our reservations online, pay the bill with our smartphone, and contact the restaurant in advance to let them know we're celebrating a special event so they can surprise us with a special gesture. In fact, we might regard these digital capabilities as a pleasant blend of human-led and digital-led customer service. On one hand, we would continue to enjoy the social and psychological benefits that come with human interaction. On the other hand, digital technology would enable us to dispense with the less pleasant aspects of the experience more quickly.

That said, there is a good reason why we "qualified" our *yes*. In the restaurant, significant parts of the customer journey cannot be easily scaled—if they can be scaled at all. For example, while some customers may be happy using digital tech to facilitate reservations and payments, others might prefer to walk through the door without a reservation and pay their bill at the cashier's station. Satisfying both customer segments would require that the restaurant continue employing a cashier or a host, despite the added cost. And unless the owner were willing to install a buffet, customers seeking self-service would have to go elsewhere.

Why are we talking about restaurants in a book about Customer Success?

It's because the restaurant is a good analogy for the dilemma that many SaaS companies and Customer Success (CS) organizations are struggling to resolve—how to deliver, more efficiently and at scale, a Human-First customer experience using digital means.

Informed by the speed, convenience, and seamlessness of their transactions with business-to-consumer (B2C) ecommerce retailers such as Amazon and Spotify, business-to-business (B2B) customers are increasingly demanding a speedier, more seamless, and more personalized experience when they purchase products and services from companies like yours. But however much you may want to fulfill your customers' wishes for "the B2C experience," achieving that goal is easier said than done.

For starters, unlike one-time purchases of books and AAA-battery 12-packs on Amazon, complex B2B SaaS products require that you and the customer devote considerable resources to onboarding new users—a process that (you hope) will lead to widespread product adoption, which, in turn, will help the customer achieve their desired business outcomes. If the customer succeeds in achieving their outcomes while having a pleasant experience, *you* succeed. You transform a one-time purchase into a subscription that generates revenue for years to come.

Turning one-off purchasers into long-term customers—customers who then buy more products and services from you, as well as advocating on your behalf—is the "prime directive" of every CS organization.

Now for the dilemma.

Most CS organizations and Customer Success Managers (CSMs) are neither prepared nor equipped to deliver the personalized customer experience their customers want, at least not in a way that is cost-effective and scalable.

Although the tools for achieving this goal *are* available—in the form of new and emerging digital technologies—most SaaS companies are stuck. They are trapped in a twilight zone between CS systems and processes that are either completely automated and impersonal or completely human-led and unscalable.

And never the twain shall meet.

In fact, some CSMs maintain (to paraphrase *Anna Karenina*) that because "happy customers are all alike, but every unhappy customer is unhappy in their own way," the entire concept of Digital Customer Success (Digital CS) is oxymoronic. In their view, SaaS firms can opt either for robotic, dehumanized interactions with their customers (a "tech-touch" approach) or for strictly human-led interactions (the "high-touch" approach). However, because every customer and stakeholder is unique, no "robot" could possibly deliver the personalized CS interactions that today's customers crave.

Use cases closed.

Never mind that not every customer is seeking a Human-First experience at every moment or a digital-first experience at every moment. Like the customers of our hypothetical restaurant, most of your customers are seeking human interactions at certain times and digital interactions at others. Thus, the *Anna Karenina* argument is a straw man argument. The human versus digital conundrum cannot be solved with either/or thinking. It can be resolved only by harnessing technology to design an optimum blend of digital *and* human CS motions for all your customers.

Technology has evolved a great deal over the past decade, and because of this, we now have a third CS model to consider—a model that can provide a personalized, human experience via digital-first methods. For this reason, we believe every company should now be thinking about *how* (not whether) to deliver a digital-first customer experience. But before we dive into this topic, let's briefly recap how we arrived at the current crossroads—the intersection of the Human-First and digital-first approaches to growth and profitability.

How We Got Here

From the moment the SaaS industry was born, it was probably inevitable that Customer Success (or something very much like it) would be invented. As soon as consumers were able to purchase, install, and use new software solutions *without* first having to wave goodbye to a substantial up-front investment, a third era of economic history had begun.

As Nick argued in *The Customer Success Economy*,[1] the first economic era was the "making stuff" phase, which started with the Industrial Revolution. The second era was the "selling stuff" phase, which was disrupted and accelerated when the internet made it possible to sell stuff globally. From 1900 to 2000, making and selling stuff was the business model of pretty much every major corporation, and it drove the global economy. A sale was a one-time activity, and anything "post-sale" represented a cost to the company.

We are now in a third phase. Although we still need to make and sell things, that is no longer enough. In the modern economy, customers are seeking success. They are seeking to achieve their goals, not just stuff to purchase. Therefore, helping customers realize their goals is now an imperative for many makers and sellers.

This new focus on desired business outcomes is why CS came into being. As companies moved from one-time sales and perpetual license agreements to recurring revenue models such as SaaS, subscription, and cloud, the power dynamics between sellers and buyers shifted (almost overnight) from sellers to consumers. Customers are no longer wedded to the vendors they bought because technology has transformed the software category for customers. They have choices. They have mobility and lower switching costs. They are the center of the SaaS solar system.

In sum, customer expectations are higher, customer power is greater, and holding onto customers is harder. (Moreover, as SaaS products become more complex, customers who are not properly onboarded or continually counseled and supported are likely to become frustrated, resulting in lower adoption rates, lower usage rates, and higher churn.)

Today, customers aren't merely asking to be "satisfied" and have "great experiences." They want to achieve their goals—and they expect *you* to help them do it for as long as it takes, even as those goals change over time. As a result, sellers and buyers have moved from largely transactional interactions to mutual, lifelong journeys. To ensure that the average journey lasts longer than a trip from your living room to the kitchen, you must cultivate strategic relationships with everyone who has a stake in ensuring that customers' business outcomes are achieved.

Because customers have changed the way they think about software vendors, you need to change your behavior if you want to keep them. You need to make sure they are actually using what they bought from you and getting the value they seek, that you're giving them the customer service they want, and that you're always looking for opportunities to expand the relationship.

Achieving these objectives is why Customer Success was invented.

At Gainsight, we define Customer Success as the concept of achieving business growth through a customer-focused approach. We strongly believe that investing your company's time, money, and effort *solely* on the acquisition of new customers is a mistake. A sales-only focus will not bring you the long-term results you desire. To attain durable growth and profitability, you must focus on retaining your existing customers, expanding your sales to them, and transforming them into fiercely loyal brand advocates. The secret to achieving all of this is making sure your customers enjoy the experience you have promised. Toward this end, everyone in your organization must collaborate to:

- Put customer needs at the core of everything, including the product roadmap.
- Develop healthy and productive customer relationships.
- Deliver an engaging customer experience.
- Focus attention on meeting customer expectations.
- Develop and track metrics that measure the customer's progress toward their desired business outcomes via the use of your products.

From Churn Busters to Revenue Boosters

As recently as 10 years ago, dropping the term *Customer Success* in the presence of a tech company founder, executive, or investor would probably have produced some puzzled looks. In 2013, when Gainsight was launched, CS was practiced by only a few dozen early SaaS companies, and you could have fit every CSM in the world on a single Boeing 747.

Since then, the number of CSMs has risen from roughly 500 to 250,000, and Customer Success is now well defined or present in 95 percent of high-growth companies.[2] And most of these firms aren't simply paying lip service to CS by squeezing a few people into a makeshift call center. They are employing skilled CS professionals by the hundreds to scale their businesses and increase net customer retention, expansion, and advocacy in the hope of increasing gross revenue retention (GRR) and net revenue retention (NRR).

Whereas many SaaS firms once struggled to understand why Customer Success even mattered, wondering "Why is this a thing?" most companies now get it. They understand, as Gartner recently reported, that

Customer Success Management is a crucial function for organizations with recurring revenue streams . . . [Customer Success Management] programs have become the standard enabler for businesses . . . to encourage customers to remain engaged and increase customer lifetime value for products sold via a subscription model.[3]

Forrester Research has concluded that "a well-designed Customer Success program can yield a 91% return on investment over a three-year period [by means of] improved customer retention, increased cross-sell and upsell opportunities, great new customer conversion rates and reduced customer support costs."[4]

Over the past decade, most SaaS firms have answered the basic questions about CS: What exactly does Customer Success mean? What type of people do you need? What other resources, technologies, and processes should you assemble to launch an effective CS program? If a company is still asking *why* or *what*, it is behind the curve. Today, most SaaS firms are focusing on *how* questions, such as:

- How do I scale Customer Success?
- How do I operationalize Customer Success?
- How do I measure Customer Success?
- How do I optimize my expansion?

This shift—from *why* and *what* questions to *how* questions—illustrates the amazing speed at which Customer Success has matured. In 10 years, CS has evolved from a purely reactive function, whose practitioners often relied on intuition and assumed best practices, into an increasingly proactive, consultative, strategic, and data-driven discipline—a discipline that has become foundational to the success of thousands of companies.

CS has progressed from call-center personnel responding to help requests and trouble tickets into CSMs who proactively collaborate with customers, as well as with Sales, Marketing, Product, IT (and more), to design, execute, measure, and monitor customer journeys that deliver the greatest possible value in the shortest possible time frame. CS has metamorphosed from a function focused on reducing churn—by promoting product adoption, addressing customer complaints, and forwarding requests for new features—into a function responsible for growing revenues by ensuring that every customer achieves their business goals via the product.

A decade ago, CS largely consisted of small firefighting squads whose members scrambled to rescue at-risk accounts on an ad hoc basis.

Today, equipped with new digital tools and data-driven methodologies, the best CS teams are intentional, proactive, strategic, and predictive, tracking leading indicators and lagging outcomes to improve revenue retention *and* growth.

CS Has Become a Company-Wide Imperative

One sign of how far CS has evolved is the accelerating recognition among SaaS executives, investors, and consultancies that Customer Success is a company-wide imperative—a core philosophy of how companies do business. Gone are the days when CS teams operated as a siloed function that "did stuff" to keep customers from eloping with competitors. These days, CS is widely viewed as a strategic pillar of the overall business—a means by which a customer-centric mindset is transformed into a durable growth engine. There is awareness that everything must be driven by the voice of the customer because, in a subscription model, you're constantly earning (or losing) customers' business.

One result of this newfound awareness and recognition is the confidence many business leaders are displaying vis-à-vis their investment in CS, even in an unfavorable business climate. According to a 2023 survey by Bain & Company (Used with permission from Bain & Company).[5]

- Although CS organizations saw increased budget pressure and slower growth during 2022 and early 2023, when CS headcount reductions *have* occurred, they have typically been in line with—or below—the reductions to broader company headcount. In fact, 75 percent of surveyed companies reported that CS *gained*, or at least maintained, its share of total company headcount.
- Most firms now consider CS a net revenue-generator, not a cost center. Unsurprisingly, firms that consider CS a cost center are more

likely to make cuts to CS (30 percent) compared with those that consider it a net revenue-generator (15 percent).

- Monetizing CS is growing in popularity. Thirty percent of the surveyed companies offer paid CS coverage, with an additional 20 percent likely to introduce a paid tier in the next three years. Of the companies that currently offer unpaid, attached CSM coverage, 35 percent expect to begin charging in the near term.

Another sign of the growing importance and respect accorded to CS is the growing number of Chief Customer Officers (CCOs) who have been elevated to the CEO position in recent years, including Yamini Rangan, CEO of Hubspot, and Christina Kosmowski, CEO of LogicMonitor.

Escape from the Twilight Zone

That brings us back to the twilight zone in which many SaaS companies find themselves today—trapped between fully automated and fully human-led CS paradigms.

Why should you care if you're stuck in this zone? Why shift to a third CS model that provides customers with a personalized, human experience, delivered by digital-first methods?

You should care because, in the wake of the SaaS industry's recent troubles, executives and investors have concluded that *durable business growth* is the key to long-term success. And which business function is best suited to play the role of the durable growth engine, given its track record of boosting customer retention, expansion, and advocacy? Customer Success. A well-oiled CS organization—one that is efficient, scalable, proactive, and data driven (but with a human face)—can be a revenue-generating machine.

There's just one problem. Relatively few CS orgs currently qualify as efficient, scalable, proactive, and data driven. Although many are dabbling with digital tools and tactics, most are taking an ad hoc approach, leveraging multiple tools and struggling to incorporate useful data because that data is siloed and/or scattered across multiple functions. The result? A disjointed customer experience, overlapping communications, and inefficiencies across the board.

Unsurprisingly, customers are frustrated with these uncoordinated experiences. And often, the people serving those customers are frustrated because they can't deliver the great experience the customer was promised. They want to do a great job, but they are stretched too thin because the current systems are manual and (often) not designed for the tasks at hand. So, your employees are frustrated, your customers are frustrated, and your investors are frustrated.

Another obstacle blocking the escape route from the twilight zone is the difficulty some CS teams are having in shifting from *defensive* strategies, especially those based on gut feelings and assumed best practices, to *offensive* strategies tethered to advanced analytics. Put bluntly, CS leaders need to accelerate the transition from squishy and artisanal relationship-management practices to practices that are scientific, data driven, and industrialized, practices that can be readily replicated and scaled. CS players who are in the vanguard of this transition are already achieving remarkable things with data analytics.

For example:

> One vendor scanned hundreds of variables using feature-discovery algorithms and found that a single metric, the three-month moving average of customer storage usage, strongly predicted which users would discontinue services within six months. Another vendor mined its customer data using machine-learning techniques to identify subsegments with the highest propensity to make a purchase and created triggers to alert them when customers entered this category. By integrating these insights into its customer-success efforts, the vendor increased customer engagement and ultimately obtained a five percent uplift in sales.[6]

For a CS leader, this is the promised land—being able to show that your team is strategic and metrics driven; demonstrating that you're not merely reactive firefighters but proactive navigators steering customers on their value journey. You're leading them to renew, leading them to expand, and turning them into advocates who help bring in new logos. And you're able to *prove* this to senior management, as well as your Sales, Marketing, and Product colleagues, by connecting the dots from your team's activities to the leading indicators and lagging outcomes.

Historically, CS leaders have not used the kinds of metrics-based business tracks that other revenue leaders employ to justify their activities and construct narratives that assign them credit for their good work.

This needs to change.

CS can no longer afford to be squishy. As a growth engine for your business, it can no longer rely solely on relationship-building techniques, customer sentiment, and guesswork. CS must become industrialized, managed with the same level of operational rigor and predictability as Sales and Marketing.

The Peloton Paradigm

Because the preferences of B2B consumers are being driven by their B2C experiences, we've searched for B2C models that optimize the digital-human mix in ways that will meet, or exceed, the evolving expectations of SaaS customers. As it happens, we have found just such a model. And it takes the form of what, at first glance, appears to be a souped-up exercise bike.

Peloton and other digital fitness companies like it have changed the way millions of people exercise. As an extremely amateur Peloton rider himself, Nick has seen, firsthand, how the company has transformed the fitness industry. Whether he chooses to ride with the inspirational Ally Love or the hilarious Cody Rigsby, Peloton has revolutionized his personal fitness routine. It has also changed how both of us think about Customer Success.

How did people work out before companies like Peloton burst onto the scene? It seemed like there were only two routes. On one hand, you had highly self-motivated people who woke up at 5 a.m. and headed straight to the gym for their personal workouts. They didn't need a coach. They didn't need a nudge. They seized the day, every day.

On the other hand, you had people with the flexibility and resources to hire a personal trainer. The trainer would coach them; design a workout routine for their body, lifestyle, and goals; and motivate them to keep at it every week.

What Peloton observed, however, was that millions of people didn't fit neatly into either of these categories, including those who:

- Want to exercise but need a nudge of encouragement.
- Want instruction, but don't have the time or resources for one-on-one training.
- Want to work out in the comfort of their homes but don't want to feel isolated.

In many ways, Customer Success has sprung from the same dichotomy. In the older business model, you had two types of clients. You had your larger clients for whom you would do anything, including customizing your software. You were like their personal "software" trainer. Then you had your smaller clients. Regardless of whether they were motivated to "go to the gym" (use your software), they still paid you, so it was all good. In addition, many SaaS companies gave their large customers a high-touch CS experience while giving the small customers a fully digital one. But this approach no longer works. Growing numbers of high-touch customers want parts of the experience to be digital, and many smaller customers want parts of the experience to involve a human. Moving forward, you will need to be more dexterous about your segmentation strategies at both the customer and persona level.

Digital Customer Success is about using process and technology to better serve *all* your customers. One way that Peloton does this is through One-to-Many "Fitness Success," which leverages the best "CSMs" (or Fitness Success Managers) in the world. These experts are inspirational. They motivate you. They entertain you. You couldn't imagine better personal trainers—and most of us could never access them one on one.

So what did Peloton do? They figured out how to scale these personal trainers to millions of people. Although the company's hardware—a connected bike with a nice screen—is a commodity, Peloton created a software platform with personalization in the form of choice and scheduling (and more) to connect the right Fitness Success Manager to the right clients.

Similarly, modern Customer Success is no longer just about high-touch CSMs for your largest clients. Leading CS organizations are creating scaled or digital initiatives, which combine strategies such as:

- Automating routine tasks like reporting, Quarterly Business Review decks, emails, and more to allow CSMs to cover more clients.
- Creating a virtual CSM through a digital-first journey based on customer behavior.
- Creating pooled CSM teams that aren't assigned to specific clients but instead intervene based on risk or opportunity triggers.

Peloton also creates personalized product experiences. The geniuses at this company realized that people don't always do what trainers want. Therefore, you sometimes need to encourage them. But the instructors can't communicate with every rider one on one, so Peloton uses the power of personalization to drive people toward the behaviors needed to achieve their goals—like noticing when you hit milestone rides and recommending rides based on your past interests. The company tracks all your habits and uses this data to ensure that you continue improving and engaging with the platform.

Finally, Peloton created a community. Although you may be physically alone on your bike, you never *feel* alone. You can join hashtag groups, compete on leaderboards, and give each other high fives. This makes you feel like you're riding alongside many other people.

The Time Has Come for CS to Reinvent Itself

The time has come for Customer Success to reinvent itself with an approach like Peloton's. The approach will embrace a custom blend of digital-first and Human-First strategies and use cases to increase the efficiency, effectiveness, and scalability of CS operations.

Already, SaaS businesses are exploring and adopting new ways to deliver more efficient and more scalable Customer Success. They include the use of in-app guides to onboard new customers, walkthroughs to help clients try out new features, and surveys to obtain feedback from customers as they work—all in the service of improving and personalizing customer experience based on users' behavioral data. We are making progress, but we need to speed things up.

To do that, businesses and CS organizations must first realize that not every customer is looking for a human touch every day. You must understand that, at any given point in the vendor-customer relationship, users may want to talk with a human or they may prefer to self-serve. They may want content dripped via email, or they may prefer a choice of walkthroughs. As a new user, you may want to talk with a human CSM 100 percent of the time, but as you gain experience, you might prefer digitized learning journeys most of the time. Yes, every customer is different in their own way, but that is not a good argument for a strictly human-led approach to Customer Success. Quite the opposite: It strengthens the argument for a hybrid approach. There are many different paths to the mountaintop, and Digital CS allows you to present each path to your clients and then let them choose which ones to follow.

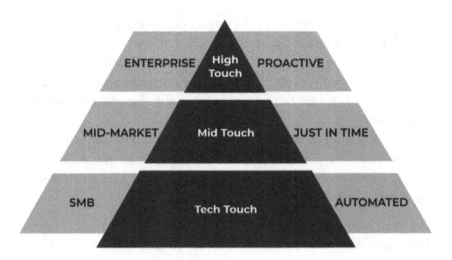

Figure 1.1   In the old Digital CS model, big customers got the human touch while small customers got tech touch.

The traditional model of Digital CS segments the market into big customers and small customers. Big customers get the human touch, and small customers get one-to-many emails. (See Figure 1.1.)

This is no longer the correct approach—if it ever was. The right approach is the one that optimizes the customer experience *and* their ability to reach their desired business outcomes, right now. In the future, we believe many customer journeys might look something like Figure 1.2.

The journey starts with a welcome email, of course, but when users log on for the first time, they see an in-app guide about how to use the product. It walks them through the steps of setting up everything, and because it notices what the user is doing, it can recommend future actions they may want to take. For example, the product may observe that the user turned on a particular feature—to which it responds by sending an email about that feature. Then the product may notice that the customer is focused on generating more revenue—to which it will respond with additional content tailored to that goal. Very likely, the customer will also be invited to connect with other customers on your Community platform. This will enable them to share experiences and learn from other customers about how to generate more revenue.

A few weeks later, your digital tech might notice that the customer stopped using the product. Are they confused? Frustrated? Thinking of

DIGITAL ENABLES DYNAMIC SEGMENTATION

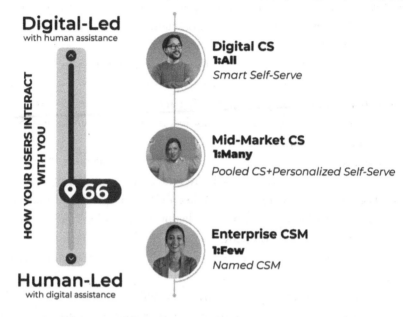

Digital-Led
with human assistance

HOW YOUR USERS INTERACT WITH YOU

9 66

Human-Led
with digital assistance

Digital CS
1:All
Smart Self-Serve

Mid-Market CS
1:Many
Pooled CS+Personalized Self-Serve

Enterprise CSM
1:Few
Named CSM

Figure 1.2 **The new Digital CS model optimizes every customer's experience through a blend of human- and digital-led motions.**

abandoning the product? You need to get them back onboard, so a CSM contacts the client to learn what the problem is. Once the problem is resolved and the customer is using the product again, a welcome-back email is automatically sent. Next month, the user might receive an infographic displaying all the revenue they have generated since they began using the product again: "Congratulations! You're doing great things with the product!"

For those of you who use Spotify, this journey may seem familiar. As a user of the music app, you receive personalized lists of song recommendations, which you can share with friends and family. Spotify also generates a personalized playlist and tells you what you have been listening to over the past year, including your favorite albums. Spotify seems to *know* you as a person.

Consider what the previous scenario would mean for the CSM assigned to the customer. Thanks to the power of Digital CS, the CSM no longer has to spend hours on Zoom, training customers how to use the product. Neither will they have to send the customer a guide on how to set up the software or (later) nudge them into using it because they haven't yet logged in. Instead, the CSM can get on the phone with the customer to focus on higher-value topics. "What are your goals going forward? What are you trying to accomplish this week or next month?"

The CSM is happier because they are devoting time to higher-value activities. The customer is happier because they are getting more value—through a combination of human touch and digital self-service. Your company is happier because it is spending less money while enabling CSMs to serve more customers.

Even without a dedicated CSM assigned to their account, the customer will feel that your company really knows them. In turn, this will increase the likelihood of them saying "I want to keep using this product. In fact, if this company has more to sell to me, I'm happy to take a look because I really love working with this company."

You're keeping the customer happy, and, as a result, you're making more money.

Until recently, we expressed this result with the formula CO + CX = CS (Customer Outcomes + Customer Experience = Customer Success). Today, with the incorporation of digital-first, we have revised the formula to this:

$$CS^D = CO^D + CX^D$$

Looking forward, your CS organization has an immense opportunity—the chance to reinvent itself with digital tools, strategies, and tactics that, in turn, present you with the opportunity to reinvent your entire company. Digital CS is not just about doing more with less; it's also about liberating your human talent to focus on motions that produce a bigger impact on your bottom line. Digital CS enables your company to extend its reach beyond the impact of individual CSMs (who are often tied to just a few key stakeholders in the customer's organization), allowing you to amplify your company-wide efforts and reach more users. In fact, we believe that every CS organization in the future should provide customers with a digital-first blend of monetized/productized services, enabling CSMs to take on more revenue-generating responsibilities.

Toward that end, this book is a detailed how-to guide to Digital Customer Success—the strategies, systems, processes, and programs you need to help your customers, your investors, and your teammates succeed. By conferring digital superpowers on your CSMs and your entire organization, you'll be well positioned to increase your NRR at a time when customer expectations have never been higher and customer retention has never been harder.

Gainsight's New Laws of Customer Success

1. Build Customer Success into your core.
2. Create an integrated customer journey.
3. Constantly drive more value or expect churn.
4. Scale with digital.
5. Drive efficiency with community and/or customer hub.
6. Leverage product and customer education to accelerate time to value.
7. Invest in Customer Success operations.
8. Deeply understand net revenue retention.
9. Ensure your Customer Success strategies are metrics driven.
10. Maintain a Human-First approach.

Summary

As business leaders, we recognize that we must scale in order to build our companies, and the way to do this is through automated systems and processes. At the same time, we also need to enhance the customer experience. We need to deliver, more efficiently and at scale, a Human-First customer experience using digital means.

Currently, most CS organizations are neither prepared nor equipped to deliver the personalized customer experience their customers want—not in a way that is cost-effective and scalable. Although the tools for achieving this goal *are* available, most SaaS companies are trapped in a twilight zone between CS systems and processes that are either completely automated and impersonal or completely human-led and unscalable.

Although many companies are dabbling with digital tools and tactics, most are taking an ad hoc approach, leveraging multiple tools and struggling to incorporate useful data because that data is siloed and/or scattered across multiple functions. The result? A disjointed customer experience, overlapping communications, and inefficiencies across the board.

Another obstacle is the difficulty some CS teams are having in shifting from *defensive* strategies based on assumed best practices to *offensive* strategies tethered to advanced analytics. CS leaders need to accelerate the transition from artisanal relationship-management practices to practices that are scientific, data driven, industrialized, and scalable.

The time has come for Customer Success to reinvent itself, exploring and adopting new ways to deliver more efficient and more scalable CS. They include the use of in-app guides to onboard new customers, walk-throughs to help clients try out new features, and surveys to obtain feedback from customers as they work—all in the service of improving and personalizing customer experience based on users' behavioral data.

We are making progress, but we need to speed things up.

2

Durable Business Strategies to Fuel Long-Term Success

According to the philosopher Heraclitus, "Change is the only constant in life."

This is one of those adages with which everyone agrees in principle, but rarely heeds in practice. Instead, most of us habitually believe that tomorrow will look pretty much like today. And it usually does. Until it doesn't.

No matter how many times the economy is disrupted by wars, new technologies, inflation, or (most recently) a worldwide pandemic, many business leaders respond—time after time—by hunkering down, cutting budgets, and looking forward to the day when everything returns to "normal." Which it never does. Things never return to exactly the way they were.

As we write this, the SaaS industry is undergoing sudden change. After watching a 12-year bull market recede in the rearview mirror, we find ourselves hurtling down a pothole-lined highway to an uncertain destination. A new era has arrived. Almost overnight, unprecedented prosperity was replaced by stagnating sales, declining valuations, and an investment community that now measures success in terms of sustainable profits rather than meteoric growth.

In 2022, tech stocks fell more than 30 percent, due to higher interest rates, higher inflation, and turbulent economic conditions.[1] By year's end, tech companies had shed more than 140,000 jobs, with many more layoffs to come.[2] In 2019, rapid growth was the key metric by which investors valued SaaS businesses. Since then, the script has been flipped. Today, durable growth is the most important valuation metric.

If, in this era of economic climate change, your once-fertile markets have turned to desert, you need to be hyperfocused on ensuring that life within your oasis of existing customers is thriving. Instead of battening the hatches and waiting for things to return to normal, you need to direct more effort—right now—to customer retention, advocacy, and expansion to achieve sustainable growth.

At a time when every customer in your bucket really counts, the last thing you need is a leaky bucket. So, given the likelihood that your firm will acquire fewer logos in the near term, you must do everything possible to persuade your current customers that they should not only renew their subscriptions but *increase* their spend with you.

To do this, you need to offer customers as much perceived value as possible. You need to double down on your Customer Success efforts to ensure that your clients will go to the mat for you if their Chief Financial Officers (CFOs) start seeking ways to cut spending. In an uncertain and volatile world, a world in which customers are taking a *very* hard look at their software spend, you want to be the company that is delivering *results*—through how well your product is adopted *and* by the role it plays in helping customers achieve their desired business outcomes.

By investing in the success of your installed base, you position your firm to experience growth that is both dramatic and sustainable. Some of the fastest-growing SaaS companies already know this. According to the fifth annual *Growth Index* of Edison Partners, SaaS companies with annual growth rates of 30 percent or more:

- Invested six times more in building their Customer Success teams than those with lower growth rates
- Grew annual recurring revenue (ARR) within their existing accounts by 35 percent

- Retained revenue at a rate 17 percent higher than their slower-growing competitors
- Achieved a net retention rate (NRR) of 102 percent

CS Is a Durable Growth Engine

Even before the downturn, many subscription-revenue companies had begun putting more emphasis on risk management and the need to deliver better experiences and outcomes for customers. This was a response to evolving technologies and consumer preferences as well as to market saturations and low switching costs. Even then, the trend lines were pointing toward growth that was more efficient, in terms of human and financial capital, and away from the growth-at-any-cost approach that characterized the previous decade.

The big question, of course, was how to achieve sustainable growth.

This is where we enter the picture. To give you the support you need to thrive during good times, bad times, and any stage of maturity, we have developed a Durable Business Playbook, which contains six proven strategies to help CS, Sales, and Product teams improve their collaboration and direct their collective energies to improving retention, expansion, and advocacy.

Please note that these strategies are not break-glass-in-case-of-recession measures that you should immediately discard as soon as the klaxon horns go silent. These are *key foundational pillars* on which every subscription-based firm should permanently rest.

Strategy #1: Avoid Surprises

If you manage a recurring revenue business and don't have your pulse on what customers are thinking, feeling, and doing (and *not* doing)—if you haven't developed a reliable customer health score and risk management process—you're in trouble. These are the table stakes for survival in today's hypercompetitive environment. Without them, you'll be in the same position as the mathematician who challenged 1, 3, 5, 7 and 9 to a boxing match.

The odds will be against you.

Math jokes aside, recent history has made one thing very clear: Although you can't prevent unexpected changes triggered by people, institutions, and events beyond your control, you *can* prevent unpleasant changes triggered by your own customers. That's why the first step of the playbook is to avoid surprises by getting serious about risk and renewal management. This should be a core tenet of your CS operations.

Your first step should be to develop a No Surprises Framework that provides *data-driven* early-warning signals from your customer base. Start by asking: "What are we doing well? Where are things off track?" and "What are we going to do about it?" These questions will help you prioritize your efforts and investments to ensure that customers who need the most attention are getting it.

At Gainsight, we leveraged our CS platform to develop a health scoring framework called DEAR (for **D**eployment, **E**ngagement, **A**doption, and **R**OI).

DEAR directs your focus to:

- **Deployment:** Is the customer activated? Are they set up to effectively use what they bought? (Poor Deployment is often a strong risk indicator for partial churn or downsell.) To determine if the customer is activated, you need accurate entitlement data (what they are licensed for) versus what they've actually activated (assigned licenses for). You also need the ability to see this data in a system that feeds a deployment health score metric. Once that is done, your CSMs will be able to receive alerts and take action if the deployment isn't reaching a desired threshold. (Poor deployment is an early-warning signal of potential shelfware.)

- **Engagement:** Is the customer engaged? Are you multithreaded to the right stakeholders? In other words, are you talking to all the right personas at the right cadence—the people with influence over the outcomes of the partnership? Be sure to identify key personas at your customer and establish SLAs for engagement. By leveraging a Customer Success platform (CSP), you can create logic, based on the activities that are occurring, to feed your engagement health score. This will signal how strong engagement is at the customer, and trigger alerts and playbooks when things go off track.

- **Adoption:** Is the customer using your product in breadth and depth? ("Breadth" refers to how often, or how many, users regularly log in and display healthy usage. "Depth" is about adoption quality— the regular use of sticky features that indicate engagement in meaningful, end-to-end workflows.) Telemetry data is becoming mission critical in SaaS for understanding how customers are using your products and where you can make improvements to drive better outcomes. Once you obtain a product adoption tool to provide you with rich data, you can feed your adoption health scores with associated playbooks based on the signals you receive.
- **ROI:** Is the customer achieving value based on the outcomes you have identified and the work you have done? The first step to value realization is creating a mutual success plan with the customer to identify their desired business outcomes as well as the key initiatives on which you will collaborate to achieve the agreed-upon success criteria. This mutual success plan should automatically drive an ROI health measure based on the completion of a verified outcome.

DEAR aims to not only help CS teams deliver exceptional customer experience, but also to drive existing customers to their desired outcomes, again and again, giving you a stickiness that will yield sustainable growth in the installed base.

In addition to a customer experience score, DEAR provides a customer outcomes score. This is an objective indicator of whether the customer is achieving value and ROI. Essentially, the DEAR customer outcomes score enables you to connect specific workflows to specific leading indicators to specific lagging outcomes. It allows you to measure every activity that your team is performing, helping you determine how those activities are impacting your business today and how they are likely to impact your business tomorrow.

Although they seem simple, these elemental analyses—performed continuously—can keep you from encountering moments with your customers when you feel like the rug has been pulled out from under you. And remember, anyone who engages with your customer—including CS, Sales, and Product—must be involved in managing risk.

Strategy #2: Scale through Digital CS

When the pressure is on to quickly and consistently deliver value (and when is it *not?*), your CS organization needs sophisticated digital tools to bring an elevated level of service to the *entire* customer base. CS promotes customer-led growth, increasing your Net Revenue Retention (NRR) by upselling and cross-selling existing customers. It also transforms customers into advocates for your product—via online communities and in-person sales/marketing events—helping to reduce customer acquisition costs (CAC).

When building out the sales function, a common mistake made by start-ups and early-stage companies is to simply throw bodies at the scaling challenge. But when it comes to building out CS, companies tend to over-correct. They try to accomplish too much with too few people. At best, this produces lackluster results and contributes to higher rates of employee burnout and turnover.

A Digital CS platform enables you to do more with less, while delivering the kind of personalized customer experience—the right message to the right customer at the right time—it takes to achieve sustainable success. Digital tools give your CS leaders time to execute more evolved operational strategies: building customer journeys and workflows using email insights; analyzing product usage to understand where your customers might be stuck; creating in-app engagements to get customers back on track; and developing a strong Community in which customers can receive peer-to-peer support.

At Okta, the leading provider of secure, cloud-based authentication solutions, Senior Manager of CS Operations Melissa Allen leveraged the Gainsight CS platform to create automated Complexity Scores for accounts, along with a Compensation Dashboard. Since it launched, this GameChanger award-winning Digital CS program has helped Okta managers assign work to the firm's CSMs in a more sustainable cadence. "It's led not only to a more balanced workload, but to a higher sentiment across the CSMs because they feel they are more accurately balanced in their account portfolio," says Allen.

The program offers the added benefit of preventing CSM burnout. "Before, many CSMs wouldn't know how to show if they were over-whelmed or exhausted from the complexity of their accounts," says Allen. "It was all rather subjective. There was no data to show if somebody was overutilized or if they were underutilized. Being able to quantify and show how your CSMs are doing also establishes transparency. There's a new level of understanding without relying on just qualitative metrics. Utilizing this scoring, you no longer have to prove what the data shows."[3]

By reducing CAC and cultivating a base of customers willing to provide low-cost assistance with your marketing, as well as Customer Support and Product Development, Digital CS is an ideal tool for boosting NRR and efficiency across business units and functions.

Going from Zero to One with Digital

Looking to improve customer experience while driving more scale, efficiency, and effectiveness in your CS motion? In a presentation at Gainsight's 2022 Pulse Conference, Jeff Beaumont, former Director of CS Operations at Gitlab, shared four basic tips on how to do so.

Define Your Purpose for Incorporating Digital

If you're only thinking about how to cut costs through digital—in other words, how to drive efficiency—that's a race to the bottom that nobody wants to win. Efficiency should not be your only goal. Obviously, efficiency is a valid objective, but if that's your singular purpose for incorporating digital into your CS motions, you'll probably find it a tough sell—to finance, sales leaders, and many others. Instead, I encourage you to think about how digital can help your organization drive *effectiveness*. For example, we were able to increase license utilization and use case adoption via digital. *That* is a far easier purpose to sell to the people in finance and sales. You may also want to create efficiencies, as well as a better customer experience, and that's fine. It's good to have multiple goals. But know what your purpose is, and know what your priorities are, from the very start.

Build Out Your Map

Knowing your purpose will help you to build out your roadmap. Where do you want to go? What do you want to be able to accomplish? And how do you get started? Beware: It's easy to get really excited about building a big roadmap—to determine, in excruciating detail, what you're going to do over time, and how you're going to solve all the world's problems. Resist this temptation. Instead . . .

Take One Bite at a Time

Eat the elephant one bite at a time, so you don't become overwhelmed. Yes, build that roadmap, but do it incrementally. Iterate through that map again and again until you finally consume the entire beast.

Choose Your North Stars

Keep in mind that whichever KPIs you set up, whichever metrics you chose—those are the North Stars toward which your team will now be oriented. That's what you're going to think about Monday morning when you come in and look at your reports. So make sure that whatever metrics you use, and whatever KPIs you set up, they are aligned with your ultimate purposes. If you want to increase license utilization and time to value for customers, that's fantastic. Those can be your metrics, as long as they are aligned with your purpose.[4]

Strategy #3: Keep the Customer in Customer Success

Given its name, the purpose of the *Customer Success* organization should be obvious. But like every other functional team, CS can sometimes wander so far into the weeds of daily demands that they lose sight of the core mission. And sometimes CSMs take an inside-out view, instead of an outside-in view, of what success means to the customer. When this happens, CSMs may fail to make the Customer Success journey a truly collaborative experience.

To leverage every expansion opportunity, SaaS companies need organization-wide strategies for acquiring customers, managing them, and driving them to *verifiable* success again and again. To achieve durable growth, it is essential that your CSMs have enough information to understand what every customer needs to reach their goals.

CSMs must take the time to genuinely understand customers' desired outcomes and then create prescriptive strategies to get them there.

To leverage every expansion opportunity, CS, Sales, and Product must collaborate with the customer to understand their goals and then execute and measure the impact of their activities on those goals.

Take the case of Shiji Group, whose guest experience management software, Shiji ReviewPro, is used by thousands of hospitality customers worldwide. Although many of their customers are large businesses that operate hundreds of locations, the company also serves a long tail of smaller businesses. For Shiji ReviewPro, this wide range of customer types posed a dilemma: Should the post-sales motion be targeted, or could a one-size-fits-all approach do the trick?

The answer came in the form of retention data. "About six years ago, we were experiencing a lot of attrition in our smaller accounts," said Neil James, Chief Operating Officer at ReviewPro. "We were very good at managing our large accounts, but we weren't doing a good job with smaller customers." The company needed scripts and process flows to make sure they were speaking to smaller customers proactively and regularly. "Our goal was to educate them as much as possible on the solutions we offered so we could reduce churn with that particular market," added James.

Using the Gainsight CS and product analytics and engagement platforms, ReviewPro was able to ramp up its digital outreach and establish a consistent, productive dialogue with smaller customers—a dialogue that led to increased engagement and reduced churn.[5]

Farther along the customer journey, the company uses Gainsight to generate upsells and assist the sales team. The process starts with customer-journey mapping by the CS team, which determines which parts of the journey will be handled by digital technology and which parts will be managed by humans. When a customer reaches a key upsell opportunity in their journey, Gainsight generates a use case (or business case). This is logged as a touchpoint type in the platform, which automatically generates use-case emails to the sales team.

At Gainsight, we've learned that customers with current, active verified outcomes will collectively generate GRR that is 12 to 15 percent higher. To facilitate this outcome, we're leaning harder into community, providing our customers with more peer-to-peer networking opportunities to share best practices and access self-service information.

Do *not* underestimate the value of community. When it comes to giving customers the ability to self-serve within a single, personalized, automated journey, there's no better tool than community-based peer-to-peer connections.

Strategy #4: Go on Offense

Because of its origins in customer support, playing defense comes naturally to many CS leaders. After all, CS was born of the need to protect your customer base, drive retention, and respond to post-sales requests. But though a good CS organization reacts quickly to requests and keeps customer sentiment high, a *great* CS organization takes a proactive stance. They know when it's time to play offense, and they know how to guide customers from adoption to renewal to expansion in a seemingly effortless, cyclical motion. When a great CS team plays offense, they work cross-functionally with Product to influence the product roadmap in ways that improve the customer experience.

It's important that you and your CS teammates are not so narrowly focused on renewals that you overlook low-hanging expansion fruit. Whatever the current business climate, it is imperative to facilitate close collaboration with the Sales, Marketing, and Product teams to unlock the expansion potential of the installed base. Joint account planning with your sales organization, supported by a data-driven way to identify customers who are ripe for expansion, is another offensive strategy that often produces great results.

At the height of the pandemic, we saw expansion dollars rise even as net new-logo acquisitions fell. To ensure that history repeats itself, strive to increase adoption of the underutilized parts of your tech stack and lean into integrated account planning to drive more Customer Success Qualified Leads (CSQLs) to your sales reps. Very often, there exists within your customer base a wealth of opportunities to gain more wallet share.

Strategy #5: Grow Through Your Product

At Gainsight, we have a saying: "CS and Product should be BFFs."

We call this the Product + CS Interlock, and while we don't take ourselves too seriously, we're very serious about this strategy.

The customer should be at the center of your universe, no matter which team you're on. CS can't solve a customer's product problem if Product isn't collaborating on a solution. So at Gainsight, one of the biggest things we've recently done is establish a customer-centric release cycle. Everyone coordinates with Product to make sure customers are ready to consume what we're preparing to ship. If we haven't hit certain milestones—indicating that customers are ready to adopt a new or enhanced feature—we hit pause until those milestones are reached.

Having a customer-centric roadmap approach like this is key to driving durable growth for your business. Infusing CS feedback and ongoing communication into the product road-mapping process ensures that your team prioritizes the right features so that customers realize value, reach their business goals, and, ultimately, become zealous advocates for your brand.

To boost customer satisfaction rates, your Product, Marketing, and CS teams should collaborate to define what customer satisfaction and product success means for each product and feature, after which they can use product analytics and engagement data to measure and track the key components of customer satisfaction, including Net Promoter Scores (NPS), Customer Satisfaction (CSAT) scores, and Customer Effort Scores (CES). Sharing this data will enable the teams to align their approach to customers and users. It will also promote agreement on product development changes, priorities, and customer-specific support to provide maximum value to your user base.

Strategy #6: Be Human-First

No matter how technical your company is, every business boils down to interactions between humans, not chatbots. In other words, your success is directly tied to the relationships you build, both with your customers and with the people in your own company. To build strong relationships, you need to behave like a human, not just your customer's CSM. This is especially true when SaaS companies are dealing with stagnant sales, downsizing, cost constraints, and other challenges. By showing up as a human with empathy and care, you will put pennies in the relationship bank that will eventually yield stronger and more sustainable relationships.

We encourage you to have fun with this strategy. For example: We send branded swag to our customers and their kids, distribute fun launch videos, and invest in programs to help new talent gain entry to the world of CS. So think of ways to surprise and delight your customers. Think of how you can create moments they will remember for the life of your relationship.

Time to Rethink Your Product Roadmap?

Implementing the Durable Business Playbook requires a fresh look at your product roadmap, because when you scale through retention and expansion, the main goal is to maximize utility for existing customers so that they will increase usage and spending. That means prioritizing core features and usability rather than adding new ones in an effort to attract new customers with adjacent use cases. With this in mind, here are four more steps that Customer Success, in tandem with Product, can take to drive durable, product-led growth.

Step 1: Get Serious About Analytics

Every business wants to use data to improve decision-making, but many fail to realize that their own product is their most potent source of that data. Product data has the power to help you understand the user journey—what users are finding useful, what they're struggling with, and how you can create value to keep them coming back for more.

That makes product analytics—data showing how your product is being used, along with user surveys, messaging, and more qualitative measures—a valuable resource as you seek to anchor your development roadmap in the things your customers actually need. Armed with user feedback, it's possible to learn how your customers feel, understand what's missing, and invest in the improvements that align with your users' evolving needs.

Step 2: Stay Focused on Stickiness

Your analytics dashboard should have a strong focus on your stickiest features. These features will include your product's key value drivers during the early evaluation stage when you're looking to hook new customers and turn their curiosity into a compelling use case for your product. But they will also include outcome-related features that enable established customers to measure and increase ROI as they scale. And they will include features that directly drive organic expansion, such as collaboration functionality that prompts users to invite colleagues to use your product.

Product managers naturally get excited about new features, but by taking a data-driven look at stickiness across the whole customer life cycle, it becomes easier to identify opportunities to innovate around your core functionality and make it more integrated, scalable, and productive. Customers won't renew or expand their contracts because you rolled out a shiny new feature. But they *will* keep renewing if your company keeps investing in making its outcome-driven features the best they can possibly be so users can be more successful at their jobs.

Step 3: Influence User Behavior

Believe it or not, most customers don't peruse your release notes in search of new features. In fact, some customers may not even notice your newly released functionality, and those who do might struggle to understand how that feature supports their core use cases or what the best practices are for using it effectively.

To increase visibility into new features, leverage in-app messaging to encourage core users to unlock the new functionality. As part of every release process, invest in user enablement by creating effective in-app communication—with links to articles and videos—that can help users to learn about, and successfully adopt, your newest features.

Step 4: Stayed Focused on Your North Star

Every SaaS business needs to focus on its North Star—on what it wants to achieve for both the customer and itself. Real resilience comes from leaning into those things and scaling by optimizing the user experience to make the product as sticky as it can be.

Building durable and resilient SaaS businesses requires a commitment to scaling through the product and using it as a vehicle to drive retention and expansion by increasing value across core features in ways that keep customers coming back for more. That, in turn, requires a fresh approach to your roadmap. More than anything else, the way you understand and invest in your product will determine your company's success or failure in the years ahead.

Make Customers the Center of Your Universe

Historically, companies in growth mode pour huge sums of cash into customer acquisition, sometimes driving CAC to ludicrous levels. In its infancy, for example, HelloFresh was said to have a CAC of \$94,[6] and the fledgling Uber once enticed prospective drivers with all sorts of incentives: signing bonuses, car loans, guaranteed hourly rates, and even free iPhones.

Eventually, every recurring revenue company will reach a stage at which new logo acquisitions decline, regardless of how many resources are poured into sales and marketing. At this point, companies will either shrink or their executives and investors will turn to retention, advocacy, and expansion to sustain profitability. Even at start-ups, existing customers can account for up to 50 percent of total revenue growth, and the cost of revenue expansion from existing customers is only a fraction of that needed to acquire a new customer.[7] In addition, leads generated by CS teams typically have the highest conversation rates.

For this reason, we strongly recommend that you adopt the Durable Business Playbook strategies as a formula to increase your wallet share of the installed base. Collectively, these six components will serve as a strategic pillar for your business, enabling you to understand what's happening within your portfolio of customers, drive increased efficiency, lower customer acquisition costs, enhance the customer experience, and ensure that everyone on your Go-to-Market (GTM) team collaborates to put the customer at the center of your universe.

Summary

Given the likelihood that your firm will—sooner or later—acquire fewer logos, you must do everything possible to persuade current customers that they should not only renew their subscriptions but *increase* their spend with you.

To do this, you need to offer customers as much perceived value as possible. In a world where customers are taking a *very* hard look at their software spend, you want to be the company that is delivering *results*—through how well your product is adopted *and* by the role it plays in helping customers achieve desired business outcomes. By investing in the success of your installed base, you position your firm to experience growth that is dramatic and sustainable.

CS organizations need to become durable growth engines. By following the Durable Business Playbook, CS, Sales, and Product teams can improve their collaboration, directing their collective energies to improving customer retention, expansion, and advocacy. The six strategies in the Durable Business Playbook are not break-glass-in-case-of-recession measures but key pillars on which every subscription-based firm should *permanently* rest.

- Strategy #1: Avoid surprises.
- Strategy #2: Scale through Digital CS.
- Strategy #3: Keep the *customer* in Customer Success.
- Strategy #4: Go on offense.
- Strategy #5: Grow through your Product.
- Strategy #6: Be Human-First.

Eventually, every recurring revenue company will reach a stage at which new logo acquisitions decline. At this point, companies will either shrink or their executives and investors will turn to retention, advocacy, and expansion to sustain their profitability.

3 | Digital Customer Success Is a Strategic Program

It was the best of times, it was the worst of times, it was the age of wisdom, it was the age of foolishness, it was the epoch of belief, it was the epoch of incredulity, it was the season of Light, it was the season of Darkness. . . .

—From *A Tale of Two Cities* by Charles Dickens

Why should you care about Digital CS?

Because Customer Success, as companies have been practicing it for the past 10 years, is no longer sustainable. We don't pretend to know exactly where the market is headed, but we *do* know that the age of growth at any cost has been supplanted by the age of durable growth. Prior to 2020, the typical CS organization scaled by throwing bodies at the challenge. It didn't matter if your company was profitable, as long as you were acquiring more customers. Today, as SaaS firms race to keep up with swiftly changing technology (especially AI) and consumer preferences, durable profits and durable growth are the yardsticks that investors use to calculate valuations and measure a company's success. If you're not profitable, forget about a high valuation.

But if CS is to serve as a durable growth engine, it must become much more efficient. And it must do that by incorporating automated processes and systems.

The subscription revenue companies that successfully deploy a Digital Customer Success (CS) approach—the companies that view CS as a revenue driver; create a CCO role; create alignment between CS, Sales, and Product; and move to an industrialized form of CS—are facing a "spring of hope." By contrast, those that continue to regard CS as a cost center; fragment their CS operations across Sales, Services, and other areas; maintain silos; and run CS as an artisanal "craft" are sledding toward a "winter of despair."

Right now, the SaaS sector is *A Tale of Two Industries*. One industry, blessed with newly acquired digital superpowers, is plotting a course direct to Heaven, while the second group—stuck in a reactive, human–only, artisanal mode—is going direct the other way.

The Quest to Scale *and* Improve Value

On the plus side, many companies are already exploring ways to scale through Digital CS. On the minus side, many are also struggling to simultaneously achieve scale while delivering real value to their customers. The following statistics illustrate just a few of the challenges that CS organizations are facing as they transition to a Digital CS model that will improve Customer Success, investor success, and teammate success:

- For quick and immediate assistance, 51 percent of consumers prefer bot interactions over human ones,[1] but according to Gartner in 2019, "only 9% of customers report solving their issues completely by using self-service."[2] These two contradictory survey results point to a troubling experience gap. Because so many users have been conditioned in the B2C environment—TikTok, Amazon, Google—to have great expectations when it comes to what good self-service and digital experiences should look like, they now expect those same experiences and self-service options with their B2B vendors. But there is currently a yawning chasm between the expectations of these customers and the realities of what B2B vendors are providing.

- Over forty percent of companies are using (at least) four to six tools for customer onboarding.[3] This is an example of needless tool proliferation. Software vendors understand that many customers are struggling to onboard their users. But how have they responded? By adding more tools. Rather than solving problems, this fix puts an even heavier burden on customers, who must now master four to six unconnected tools before they can start to address the problems these tools were designed to solve. In short, many SaaS companies have addressed customers' onboarding challenges by giving them even *more* challenges to overcome, instead of supplying a single, user-friendly solution.

All of this impacts the bottom line—yours and your customers'. When subscription revenue companies and their CS organizations try to scale via digital, but discover that their efforts are not working as well as anticipated, they often default back to manual, high-touch programs. But customers are still not reaching value from the product, which results in missing ROI, low adoption rates, and a disjointed experience. Meanwhile, your company struggles with unacceptable churn triggered by unhappy users, which results in lower NRR. If this chain of misery is not broken, it can become a vicious cycle that repeats itself indefinitely.

From Tech Touch to Bionic CSMs

Until recently, Digital Customer Success was often known as *tech touch*. It was a customer segmentation strategy (usually for the lowest-spend customers) based on the recognition that the average CS organization could not afford to scale by simply hiring more CSMs to serve both the high- and low-spend customers. Tech touch was also a cost driver that was used to scale a better customer experience across all segments, where the long tail typically did not get much (if any) human-led support.

In most cases, lower-spend customers were served with one-to-many emails, webinars, and office hours. These were the usual go-to, along with some how-to documentation on your website, designed to keep users from bombarding customer support with too many questions. At Gainsight, we even developed a graphic to illustrate the role of tech touch. As you can see in Figure 1.1, the pyramid features: your largest customers at the top, receiving high-touch service from human CSMs; a mid-touch level, which offers a mix of tech touch and human-led services for mid-size customers; and at the bottom, your small, low-spend customers, who receive a relative handful of emails, webinars, and the like and no human support.

Today we believe this approach was dead wrong. And even if it *had* been correct, several recent changes would have rendered it obsolete by now:

- Customers' desire for how they consume software has shifted. They expect more personalized and guided experiences today than they did just a few years ago.
- Technology has evolved, enabling us to better serve customers in a tailored, proactive manner (via in-app messaging, AI, product usage analytics, and more orchestrated [and less fragmented] engagements).
- Because of economic climate change, there is now a greater need to direct your human capital to only the most high-value activities. This can be done by leveraging technology and automation to scale life cycle moments that are digital-first.

The reality is that tech has changed, and so has the market. Customers, whether they are enterprise customers or SMB clients, want to engage digitally. That is their expectation. The old pyramid implied that digital approaches were only for clients you could not serve with people. Today, nearly every forward-thinking company has realized that Digital CS is valuable for *all* clients—clients that, regardless of their size, want a self-service experience; clients that have worked with you for a long time and don't need another *Quarterly Business Review*. Today's Digital CS is also better at automating routine tasks (saving time for both the customer and the CSM) and at reaching stakeholders who don't want to engage in a high-touch fashion. And from a cost perspective, you, as the vendor, should give them what they want. You cannot afford to keep recruiting more troops for the CS trenches.

We are willing to admit our mistake regarding the pyramid. As Taylor Swift says, "It's me, hi, I'm the problem, it's me." Today we fully embrace Digital CS as a solution suitable for every SaaS customer. And for a SaaS vendor, Digital CS is one of the most cost-effective growth solutions available. By deploying the right digital tools and workflows at the right time with the right messaging, you can quickly and efficiently scale your retention and expansion efforts, transforming your existing CSMs into Bionic CSMs.

By leveraging product adoption data, digital communication channels, in-app engagements and surveys, automated email sequences, workflow-driven playbooks, and a vibrant user Community, you can make every CSM better, stronger, and faster—freeing them to devote more time to high-value activities rather than repetitive low-value tasks.

Make no mistake: Incorporating digital tools is not about replacing CSMs with a fully automated Customer Success program. Rather, it's about equipping your CS team with tools that serve as force multipliers, augmenting their abilities and giving them more time to focus on strategic initiatives instead of sending the same emails again and again.

When it comes to scaling CS, you can't simply hire more bodies and hope for the best. You need a digitally enabled program that can provide customers with more personalized experiences without requiring more persons. Truth be told, many of your biggest clients want a more digital experience, while some of your smaller customers want a high-touch experience. Digital-led motions will help you to more efficiently deliver *both* types of experience.

Digital CS Defined

We define Digital CS as a strategy to efficiently drive customer adoption, retention, and growth by providing personalized user experiences via omnichannel engagement. Digital Customer Success blends digital and human interactions and empowers users to self-serve by leveraging data-driven automation and centralized resources. The goals are to drive:

- **Investor Success** with higher margins (increased efficiency while improving GRR/NRR);
- **Customer Success:** Increased ROI (seamless experience with increased value); and
- **Teammate Success:** Increased productivity, leveraging technology to enable CSMs to devote more time to high-value activities.

A well-designed Digital CS strategy will:

- **Increase Scale and Efficiency** by aligning the business around a single source of truth. It will also automate actions and orchestrate customer engagements to ensure value delivery at scale.

- **Improve Customer Retention** by acquiring a deeper understanding of your customers, enabling you to proactively guide them to value and to identify early signals of risk, effectively mitigating churn at scale.
- **Improve User Experience and Product Adoption** by analyzing usage and sentiment data to create targeted in-app engagements that drive user behaviors, deliver on feedback, and drive value and growth. Digital CS enables us to extend our reach to many more users than a CSM can engage with. This is important because, as users acquire more market power and a stronger voice, we need to help these end users adopt our software more quickly and thoroughly.
- **Increase Expansion Opportunities** through the use of predictive analytics and workflows to scale efforts around renewing and expanding successful customers, and decreasing revenue leakage.

To achieve these objectives, Digital CS leverages data—everything from integrated, AI-powered customer data and product analytics to surveys and AI-driven insights—to improve the customer journey with engagement vehicles such as communities/digital hubs, customer hubs, in-app guides, knowledge bots and surveys, automated email campaigns, and programmatic renewals, as well as pooled CS management, distributed work assignment, and CSM queues.

Digital CS is a strategy that enables your CSMs to focus on the highest-value activities by blending human and digital touchpoints that scale your existing programs and create more value for your customers.

Digital CS is *not* tech touch or low touch only, and it is *not* intended for only your SMB or low-spend customers. And it is *definitely not* designed to replace CSMs with robots that will deliver dehumanized interactions with your customers.

Digital-led CS is not at odds with human-led. In fact, the two models are mutually supportive. As CS leaders and teams incorporate digital technology into their systems and processes, they will be better positioned to give customers more of what they want—more personalized user journeys and more self-service options. Digital CS enables CSMs to do more with less. Your people will be freed to focus on higher-value activities instead of mundane and repetitive tasks, many of which can now be automated.

Although it's no coincidence that Digital CS began gathering force after the arrival of the pandemic, even before COVID-19, many companies had begun to realize that:

- Many customers were simply too small to serve economically with a high touch, human-driven model.
- Some customers—and user personas—don't want to engage in the Quarterly Business Reviews and check-in calls that are the hallmarks of high-touch CS.
- As they grow, companies need to improve their margins by growing revenues faster than the size of their CS teams.

After 2020, as rising inflation and interest rates fueled economic uncertainty, SaaS companies began seeking new ways to achieve efficient growth with their CS teams—and many now see Digital CS as the means to this end.

As Digital CS evolves from a support-ticket deflection tool into a broader CS strategy that can be applied to every customer segment, you should seek out areas where automation can augment the good work of your team. You should look for ways that digital tools and channels—from email, chat, and portal to online communities, videos, webinars, and in-app tutorials—can liberate your CSMs to devote more time to customer outcomes and time-to-value realization. From the start, however, it's important that you be clear and intentional about which activities are best performed by humans versus digital tools—and how the division of labor should be applied across segments.

Many Digital CS journeys begin with the elimination of repetitive tasks via basic self-service programs, which enable users to find answers to common questions without relying on human CS or Support. Components of automated self-service offerings often include regularly scheduled office hours sessions where users ask questions of other users and a CSM or product expert; use-support documentation and online training to help customers get comfortable with a new feature before setting up; short videos that guide users to complete common tasks; and in-app bots that offer relevant articles and ideas. These basic self-service offerings allow users to help themselves and each other, enabling you to serve more customers with fewer people.

From here, many organizations move on to scaled customer messaging, converting common customer communications into automated or semi-automated processes that increase awareness of new/improved features, events, etc.

Some organizations, including Gainsight, have also adopted a pooled CSM model. This is a cost-effective way of supporting smaller customers using a pool of CSMs who work across a large set of customers to provide a more personalized experience at scale. Very often, the pooled CSM team will also monitor customer health and data and will be ready to intervene if a customer veers off track. For example, if the early-warning data indicate a heightened risk of churn, someone from the pool can jump in and run one or more playbooks that they have keyed up, based on those signals. In sum, your pooled CSMs monitor customers, intervene when necessary, and manage a queue of incoming requests. So while you're leading with digital, the CSMs are ready to provide intervention and support as needed.

Eventually, a pooled CSM team can create a virtuous circle of Digital CS resources by becoming subject matter experts (SMEs) for specific features or best practices. Based on the common patterns in customer needs and requests, these SMEs can then develop templated resources that can be delivered automatically.

Integrating Digital CE with Digital CS

Today, smart companies are using digital to scale CS and are making CS a company-wide responsibility. At the same time, many of these companies now view Customer Education (CE) as not just a Professional Services revenue driver but also as an enabler of CS in the broadest sense. In this new vision of the future, Digital CE, which comprises programs that help onboard, engage, and retain customers at scale via Learning Management System (LMS) platforms, is seamlessly integrated with Customer Success. This makes perfect sense, given the immense amount of overlap between CE and CS. Essentially, both disciplines are about helping customers adopt behaviors that drive the business outcomes they're seeking. It's this aligned mission that makes Digital CE a natural component in the evolution of Digital CS (which is why Gainsight recently acquired Northpass, the leading CE platform).

At the moment, many B2B SaaS firms are still behind the curve when it comes to optimizing the efficiency with which they educate customers about their products and features. According to a survey conducted by Gainsight, 70 percent of B2B SaaS companies still use traditional (i.e., manual) methods of customer training, with 54 percent requiring their CSMs to personally administer the programs. However, as companies seek new ways to increase efficiency and productivity, many are looking to slash the amount of time that CS and Professional Service teams must spend on training while increasing the amount of time these teams can devote to providing more value to customers and their own businesses. This trend is helping speed the adoption of Digital CE platforms—as is the ability of these platforms to supply data-driven evidence of their value.

Until recently, many SaaS executives were reluctant to invest in Digital CE, thanks to unanswered questions about its utility—questions such as: Where does CE live in my organization? If I adopt Digital CE, will anyone use it? and How do I measure the ROI?

For a time, these unanswered questions prevented Customer Education from achieving a breakout moment. Today, those questions can be answered in *very* favorable ways.

To start, we believe that Gainsight's acquisition of Northpass firmly plants the CE function under the CCO, giving it a home with a prominent and rising executive in the world of SaaS. By integrating Digital CE into a full suite of CS, CX, customer hub, and Community platforms, SaaS companies can deliver learning experiences that are seamlessly integrated into existing customer journeys.

As for ROI, we've observed that customer education impacts three primary pillars:

- **Customer Experience:** Effective customer education programs enable customers to learn in the ways they want—personalized and on demand. The key metrics to monitor include the percentage of total customers trained, the CSAT of the training program, and the NPS of untrained versus trained customers.
- **Operational Efficiency:** A successful Customer Education program reduces costs and unlocks valuable time. The critical metrics to monitor are the time CS teams spend on manual training *before* versus *after*

investing in Digital CE, the volume of support tickets, and the amount of time that CS teams can now devote to executive relations, use case expansion, and customer advocacy.

- **Revenue Impact:** The best CE programs drive revenue growth. Here, the primary metrics to monitor are training's impact on Gross Revenue Retention (GRR) and Net Dollar Retention (NDR).

As Steve Cornwell, Gainsight SVP of Strategy for Customer Education, recently told us:

> There are already glimpses of what the future of CS will look like, thanks to its marriage with CE. Many customers have told me that before investing in Digital CE, their CS teams spent at least 30 percent of their time administering training. After investing in Digital CE, they say, "Our CSMs now spend *zero* time on training. Zero. We've fully offloaded that critical function to the CE platform and it's now running everything.[4]

What does this mean for your CSMs moving forward?

It means they'll be able to invest more time building executive relationships. It means they'll have more time to understand the priorities and challenges of their customers' businesses, allowing them to craft more creative solutions to help those companies succeed. They'll have more time to network across their customers' enterprises, finding more use cases that their products will support, which will lead to more expansion opportunities. They'll also have more time to engage their points of contact in advocacy programs, referral programs, and co-marketing programs to really drive results and shine a light on those results to boost word-of-mouth marketing. In addition, they'll be able to work more closely with their account manager counterparts on expansion opportunities.

There's a persistent misconception among SaaS leaders that CE is something for big, mature companies. Most likely, this notion dates to the era before Digital CE technology—a time when companies, after reaching a certain scale, would hire dedicated staff to educate customers. In reality, many earlier-stage organizations are badly in need of Digital CE, and thanks to modern technology, companies with just 50 or 100 employees can now afford to build these programs. Before it was acquired by

Gainsight, Northpass's customer base was mostly composed of small- and mid-market businesses.

Today, Digital CE isn't just for the big boys. It's for companies of almost any size.

Launch Your CS Program with Digital

One question we frequently hear from customers is: "How do we move from the general to the specific—from Digital CS as an abstraction to Digital CS as a concrete set of strategies, technologies, and motions? You're telling us that we have to do things differently. You're telling us about new technologies that we should incorporate. How can we do that? And what should we do if we don't have an established CS organization or even a single CSM?"

If you're thinking of building out a CS function from scratch, we *highly recommend* that you start with Digital CS, not human-led CS. You can launch a Digital Customer Success initiative without hiring a single CSM. Instead, you can assign ownership to one or more people in your Marketing or Customer Support departments.

As a first step, consider developing a web-based customer hub—a simple site to facilitate the onboarding process for new users. How can you inform all your customers and users that there is now a single place they can go for help? How can you assure them that you will continue to invest in the customer hub and that the portal will now contain every tool and piece of content they need to successfully adopt and use your product?

One answer is to build a Community platform that *also* serves as the customer hub.

When you think of a Community, an image may come to mind of groups, subgroups, and threads in which the members are encouraged to ask—and answer—questions. If you are old enough, you may recall the types of forums and chat rooms that first gained popularity during the Web 1.0 era. If so, forget about them. Today's communities are much more sophisticated. Thanks to advances in technology, you can accomplish a lot more with this tool. For example, the Gainsight Community is not just a Q&A forum but a vehicle through which we collect product feedback and sponsor up-and-down voting about proposed new features and enhancements, enabling customers to directly influence the direction of our product roadmap.

One of our customers has taken this idea a step further. Gong, a call recording and revenue intelligence platform, has leveraged Gainsight tools to develop a customer hub that not only serves as a place where users can get answers to their questions but that also offers onboarding tools and encourages advocacy. If you want to recommend Gong to a peer, their customer hub is the place to go to learn how, when, and where to do that and also to learn about the rewards you'll receive for your efforts. Thus, in addition to giving customers a forum for questions and answers, the Gong customer hub serves as an interactive hub that offers multimedia resources for onboarding, training, and advocacy.[5]

Upon launching a Digital CS program, leverage your new CS tools to deliver key use cases to customers. For example, you may want new users to first become acquainted with your product and your Community. Then, as they start the onboarding journey, you can provide hands-on guidance via in-app walkthroughs to help them reach value faster. As they learn your platform, all the documentation they need can be at their fingertips in the form of an in-app Knowledge Center bot. As they become more proficient with the product, they can be alerted to new feature announcements and walkthroughs, and can also provide customer feedback in app.

Early on, users will benefit from participating in your Community, asking questions, getting answers, submitting ideas, and ultimately becoming an advocate for your company. All your product and Community activities can be automatically tracked and synced to Customer Success, where your CSM will know exactly how well each user's journey is progressing. Not only that, but if a user deviates from the desired onboarding process (or any other path), they can be automatically steered into a blended digital- and human-touch journey, enabling your CSMs to easily monitor where product usage is waning or whether users are struggling with particular features.

Thanks to this, your CSMs can be leveraged with incredible efficiency, being brought into the process only when necessary to complement your digital motions. And this human involvement can quickly and easily be scaled up or down. Ultimately, Digital CS will enable your company to do more with less by automating, consolidating, and enabling data-driven actions that facilitate proactive monitoring and reduced churn.

Your Community as a Third Place

Starbucks once positioned itself as the "Third Place." Customers had home, they had work, and they had Starbucks—a place where they could go to get work done and take some time for themselves.

With Digital CS, you can create a Third Place that consolidates all your human- and digital-led activities in a single location. This gives your customers more value than they would receive if all your CS tools were scattered across different teams with no connection to each other, which is often the case today. Not only do you improve the user experience by bringing all these resources together for them, you also liberate your CSMs from hour after hour of brain-draining scut work. Without a Third Place, many of your CSMs would be on the hook for manually sending emails and/or making calls, about everything from onboarding sessions to new feature announcements. But once your Third Place is in place, they can devote time to highlighting the value of the Community and pushing users to self-serve by clicking on links to an entire library of multimedia content, including LMS content such as training and best-practice videos, manuals, ebooks, and blog posts. All of these things can be tailored to the users, based on their desired outcomes, use cases, maturity, and so on.

Job postings are another huge part of many communities. The ability to post and apply for jobs within the Community increases engagement by creating a sense that your company is going places, which, in turn, encourages people to come along for the ride.

Again, you don't necessarily need to have an entire CS team to build and manage the Community/customer hub. It can be done by Marketing or by a single CSM. However, you *do* need someone—someone to design, organize, and update all that content.

After you've created your Third Place and informed customers that this is where they need to go, the question becomes: "How do we keep them in the habit of going there?"

Ideally, you will do this organically—by posting resources and facilitating peer-to-peer interactions that are so helpful and engaging that users will want to return again and again without prompting. In addition, you can drive users to the Community/digital hub via your product, using in-app engagements to encourage users to take a specific next step or derive more value from whichever features they're already using.

For example, after a customer has a meeting with somebody at Gainsight using the Gainsight application, a message like this will pop up: "How satisfied are you with your recent meeting?" This allows our customers to send us a quick signal about whether we are helping them or not. Instead of sending this quick CSAT question by email and hoping the user opens it and answers the question, we increase the odds that the customer will respond by having the message pop up *within* the application.

If you were a Gainsight user in October 2022, you would have received an in-app pop-up alerting you to a how-to session about health scoring. You could do something similar, creating awareness for your digital events *within* the application while simultaneously reinforcing the message that "our Community is the place to be!" In other words, you would use in-app messaging to connect two things—a digital event and the Community. "Want to sign up for this event? Go to the Community to sign up." Or "Did you know that we just released a new training video for users like you? Watch the video in the Community."

You even do onboarding in app, purchasing this capability from a vendor, rather than having to build it from scratch with expensive engineering resources. In-app onboarding is an incredibly efficient way to create a better experience for your customers.

Where Are You on the Spectrum?

The revised version of our old tech touch diagram is no longer a pyramid, as shown in Figure 1.1. It's a spectrum (see Figure 3.1). What we are saying is this: The way you adjust your mix of digital and human experiences should be based on your customer segment and the needs of the users. Today, *everyone* is looking for digital CS experiences.

Digital CS is no longer tech touch (please banish that term from your vocabulary) or low touch only. It is not designed solely for your SMB segment, and it is not a replacement for CSMs, because the idea of talking with a robot is not something that many people relish.

Digital CS *is* about the right balance between Human-First and digital-first—and it *is* about turbocharging the efficiency of your CSMs.

HUMAN & DIGITAL PROGRAMS ARE A SPECTRUM

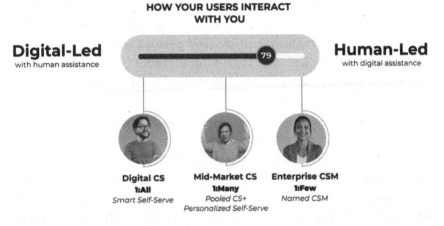

HOW YOUR USERS INTERACT WITH YOU

Digital-Led
with human assistance

79

Human-Led
with digital assistance

Digital CS	Mid-Market CS	Enterprise CSM
1:All	**1:Many**	**1:Few**
Smart Self-Serve	*Pooled CS+ Personalized Self-Serve*	*Named CSM*

Figure 3.1   In the new Digital CS model, the mix of digital-led and human-led experiences should be based on customer segment and the needs of the users.

We have a CSM at Gainsight who works with one of our largest clients, IBM, which has thousands of Gainsight users. If our CSM had to train each new user without the benefit of automation, that activity *alone* would be a full-time job. Our CSM would be saying, "Let me show you what Gainsight is and how to use it" so often that they'd be reciting those words in their sleep every night.

Testing Your Digital CS Program

To ensure a smooth transition from a fully human-led CS program to one that successfully incorporates digital, we recommend that you start with pilot programs that target low-risk situations and customers and then expand the program as you gain confidence.

To limit their exposure even more, some companies launch pilots with only their new clients in order to set expectations for the digital program from Day 1. Alternatively, you might begin by testing your program on your more technical user personas (such as system administrators)—on people who tend to be more open to a Digital CS experience.

To prevent test subjects from feeling like unappreciated lab rats, some companies offer a quid pro quo. "You work with us to test our product and give us feedback, and we will offer you the following benefits." In addition, some companies do not position their tests *as tests*. Instead of saying, "Hi, customer, we'd like you to be part of our digital-led segmentation experiment," they reach out like this: "Hi, customer. Here is your new suite of CS resources. If you need someone to help you, feel free to email [CSM name] at [email address]."

From the customer's point of view, you are giving them all these new and marvelous resources—Community, user groups, office hours. You're not ostracizing them to some digital netherworld. You aren't making them feel like they are second-class citizens who are getting a second-class experience and a third-class level of attention. Far from it! You are providing them with new and exciting ways to help them achieve their business outcomes. You are delivering an experience that is personalized and chock full of convenient self-service options.

Who wouldn't want to be a part of that?

However you choose to start, and whichever customer segments or personas you target, it bears repeating that the goal of Digital CS is not to replace human interactions with self-service or inflict an IVR-propelled spiral of misery on customers. The purpose is to leverage digital technology so that, as your company grows, the CS team can focus on providing *more* personalized service and *more* high-value communications, not less.

Summary

Customer Success, as companies have been practicing it for the past 10 years, is no longer sustainable. Prior to 2020, the typical CS organization scaled by throwing bodies at the challenge. It didn't matter if your company was profitable, as long as you were acquiring more customers. Today, durable profits and growth are the yardsticks that investors use to measure a company's success.

If CS is to serve as a durable growth engine, it must become much more efficient by incorporating automated processes and systems.

Until recently, Digital Customer Success was often known as *tech touch*. It was a customer segmentation strategy based on the recognition that the average CS organization could not afford to scale by simply hiring more

CSMs to serve both the high- and low-spend customers. Today, we believe this approach was dead wrong. And even if it *had* been correct, several recent changes would have rendered it obsolete by now:

- Customers' desire for how they consume software has shifted.
- Technology has evolved, enabling us to better serve customers in a tailored, proactive manner.
- Because of economic climate change, there is now a greater need to direct your human capital to only the most high-value activities.

Customers, whether they are enterprise customers or SMB clients, want to engage digitally. Today, nearly every forward-thinking company has realized that Digital CS is valuable for *all* clients.

A well-designed Digital CS strategy will:

- **Increase Scale and Efficiency** by aligning the business around a single source of truth.
- **Improve Customer Retention** by acquiring a deeper understanding of your customers, enabling you to proactively guide them to value and to identify early signals of risk, effectively mitigating churn at scale.
- **Improve User Experience and Product Adoption** by analyzing usage and sentiment data to create targeted in-app engagements that drive user behaviors, deliver on feedback, and drive value and growth.
- **Increase Expansion Opportunities** through predictive analytics and workflows to scale efforts around renewing and expanding successful customers, and decreasing revenue leakage.

As Digital CS evolves from a support-ticket deflection tool into a broader CS strategy that can be applied to every customer segment, seek out areas where automation can augment the good work of your team. Look for ways that digital tools and channels can liberate your CSMs to devote more time to customer outcomes and time-to-value realization. From the start, however, it's important to be clear and intentional about which activities are best performed by humans versus digital tools—and how the division of labor should be applied across segments.

If you're thinking of building out a CS function from scratch, we recommend that you start with Digital CS, not human-led CS. As a first step, consider developing a web-based customer hub—a simple site to facilitate the onboarding process for new users. The next step is building a Community platform that also serves as a customer hub—a place containing every tool and piece of content that users need to successfully adopt and use your product.

To ensure a smooth transition from a fully human-led CS program to one that successfully incorporates digital, we recommend that you start with pilot programs that target low-risk situations and customers, and then expand the program as you gain confidence.

4

The Digital Customer Success Maturity Model

Most SaaS companies are dipping their toes into digital waters, but many have not yet learned how to swim. Although a few firms have already mastered advanced strokes and styles, many are treading water, and some are flailing. Why? Because their CS strategies are still reactive and their resources are scattered. They might have one website for customer support, another containing best-practices tips, and another for customer Q&A. One CSM might have a library of training manuals stored on her computer while another is sitting on a cache of email templates. Overall, the approach is ad hoc, the strategies are reactive, and the impact on customers is suboptimal (to put it kindly). In some instances, overworked CSMs are doing a better job of inspiring pity among their customers than driving successful outcomes.

If this description sounds like your company or CS organization, you may be trapped in the twilight zone we mentioned in Chapter 1. Although you now have access to Digital CS resources, you are still in the Reactive phase and haven't yet entered the realm of true Digital CS. In the Reactive phase, CS typically responds to customer needs only *after* the customer verbalizes those needs, in an improvised fashion, and with resources that are unorganized and siloed. This produces inefficiencies and a poor customer experience. (See Figure 4.1.)

The Three P's of Digital CS Success

Based on our many customer conversations and industry analysis, we've developed a model to help SaaS companies identify, understand, and progress through the stages of Digital CS maturity, which we've labeled the Proactive, Personalized, and Predictive. (See Figure 4.2.)

- **Proactive Stage:** In this first stage of Digital CS maturity, your mission is to empower users to self-serve with centralized resources and guides.
- **Personalized Stage:** In this second phase of Digital CS, your mission is to enable distinct user journeys, automated by data, that influence successful customer behaviors. These journeys are orchestrated by data-driven, scalable, one-to-many programs that are integrated within (and around) the product.
- **Predictive Stage:** This is the apex of Digital Customer Success. By this point in your maturity, you are designing intelligent customer experiences, powered by omnichannel technologies, that *very quickly* drive customers to their desired business outcomes.

Figure 4.3 summarizes the three phases.

Proactive Phase: Get Customers to Self-Serve

The main objective of the Proactive phase is to provide customers with basic self-service—to create an efficient, pleasant experience during which they can find the right resources at the right time. At the beginning of this stage, you may not even know which customers are interested in self-service. No matter. This is something they can determine for themselves. Those who *are* interested will be empowered to self-serve with product and user-orientation resources such as:

- A **Customer Hub**, which enables you to increase customers' self-service resolution rate by establishing an all-in-one customer

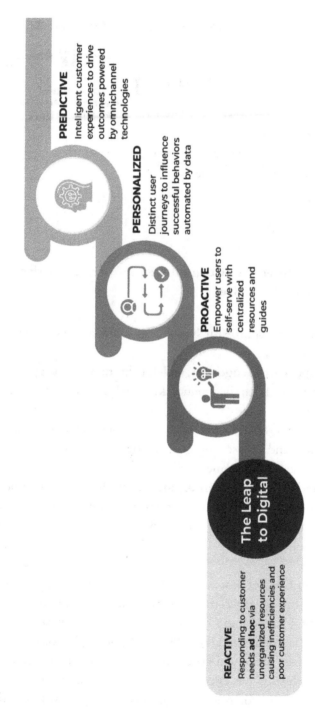

REACTIVE
Responding to customer needs **ad hoc** via unorganized resources causing inefficiencies and poor customer experience

The Leap to Digital

PROACTIVE
Empower users to self-serve with centralized resources and guides

PERSONALIZED
Distinct user journeys to influence successful behaviors automated by data

PREDICTIVE
Intelligent customer experiences to drive outcomes powered by omnichannel technologies

Figure 4.1 The Leap to Digital is a leap toward greater CS efficiency and a better customer experience.

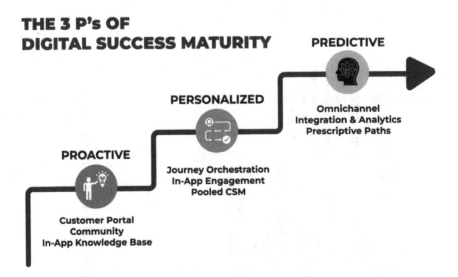

THE 3 P's OF DIGITAL SUCCESS MATURITY

PREDICTIVE
Omnichannel
Integration & Analytics
Prescriptive Paths

PERSONALIZED
Journey Orchestration
In-App Engagement
Pooled CSM

PROACTIVE
Customer Portal
Community
In-App Knowledge Base

Figure 4.2   The three P's of Digital CS maturity: Proactive, Personalized, and Predictive.

destination for resources such as videos, webinars, and other digital events.

- An **In-App Knowledge Bot**, which helps to reduce support-ticket volumes through an in-product knowledge base, guides, articles, and more.
- **Community Q&A/ Discussions**, which allow you to scale customer self-service and boost engagement by promoting peer-to-peer discussions among customers and users.
- **Federated Search and Integration**, which saves users time, and reduces incoming CS and support tickets, by offering users a way to search across your customer hub, Community, and other sources of external content.

As we saw in Chapter 3, when Gong—the call recording and revenue intelligence platform—began its transition from the Reactive to the Proactive stage of maturity, it leaned into Community to drive more meaningful participation among customers and users. Previously, although Gong customers wanted a place where they could share and learn from one another, the company's existing tech stack was disconnected, making it hard for users to find what they were looking for. And internally, maintaining cross-functionality

	PROACTIVE	PERSONALIZED	PREDICTIVE
Strategy	Empower users to self-serve with centralized resources and guides	Distinct user journeys automated by data	Intelligent experiences powered by omni-channel technologies
Use Cases	• Multi-Channel Product / Feature Awareness • Digital Events • Unified Search • Guided Self-Service • Gen. Community Programs	• Adoption Programs by Role • Closed Loop Surveys + Advocacy • Pooled CSM • Account-Based Expansion Campaigns (by Role) • Community Cohorts	• Outcome-focused Adoption Journeys • Self-Serve Value Realization • Low / No touch Renewals • Private Customer Portal
Capabilities (Gainsight Features)	• Shared 360 • NPS Email / In-App • Content Hub • Knowledge Base • Online Community • Federated Search • Product Ideas & Updates • Announcements & Events Registrations • In-App Knowledge Bot, Feedback & Announcements	• Shared Success Plans & Snapshots • Automated Email Programs • Pooled CSM Routing • Surveys & Sentiment Analysis • Role-based Landing Page • User Groups & Gamification • Paywalls and Trials • Usage-driven In-App Guides, Surveys & PQLS	• Multi-channel JO Programs • Horizon Multi-channel Analytics • Automated Renewal Process • Content Recommendations • Conversational AI
Data to Prioritize	User-level page tracking, buyer-level contact data	User-level actions plus Contact + Role Data; plus Customer Goals	Client entitlements unified w/ Goals Usage + Contacts

Figure 4.3 Although Digital CS maturity is a linear progression, your organization may eventually occupy multiple levels of maturity.

around the customer and maintaining existing workflows was a challenge for Gong's CS team. So as Gong crossed the threshold into the Proactive stage, they transformed the Community from a forum largely dedicated to Q&A into a customer hub that centralizes resources and leverages key integrations with federated search to make content easily discoverable.

As a result, 36 percent of Gong accounts are now participating in the Community, which has increased retention and product stickiness. Today, active customer hub users upsell at a rate three times higher those who are not active, according to Nisha Baxi, head of Community. "So we're tracking those numbers and seeing higher retention rates."[1]

Similarly, customers of Docebo, a SaaS company specializing in LMS, wanted a better way to connect, share best practices, ask questions, and provide product feedback. Docebo needed a solution that was intuitive and easy to implement and maintain, but one that could also grow and scale with them. To that end, the company proactively responded by driving peer-to-peer support and engagement with its Community Q&A forums, using Product Updates and Ideas to improve the way the product team engages with the customers, and by leveraging federated search to bring its Knowledge Base, Academy, and Community content together in one place.

The "Docebo Community has added value for Docebo customers that goes beyond just our products and services," says Adam Ballhaussen, former Senior Director of Customer Education and Advocacy. "Through the Community, our customers can find other like-minded individuals that can help them succeed in their roles. This ecosystem becomes an irreplaceable asset for our customers that helps drive retention and advocacy."

In less than a year, Docebo built a thriving Community in which 1,800 new product ideas were created, the peer-to-peer (P2P) response rate increased by 96 percent, and 50-plus new registrations took place every week.[2]

If you would like to follow in the footsteps of Gong and Docebo, the first step is to make all your content—from videos and webinars to onboarding guides and articles—available on your Community platform/customer hub, so that anyone searching the platforms will be able to find the information they need, easily and quickly. Fortunately, you don't need much customer data at this stage of maturity. All you need to know is who the users are and whether you can track them in your application. Although data is crucially important to Digital CS, do not let a lack of data be a barrier to getting started. You can create great digital experiences with very little data. For example: At the start of the Proactive phase, you don't necessarily need to know who the customer is and the users' roles. Your only goal is to aggregate relevant content in one place—in a way that enables your customers to self-serve.

Personalized Phase: Get the Right Information to the Right Person

Once you graduate to the Personalized phase, it's no longer a matter of simply gathering standardized resources in one place. At this point, you want to customize your resources based on what you know about different users. If the user is an administrator, you will send them a different feature release note than you would if the person were an executive or an end user. This is what we mean when we talk about adoption programs by role.

The Personalized phase makes widespread use of one-to-many programs that are designed to guide specific customers and users to value through scalable engagements. Some examples of these engagements include:

- **An Embedded Knowledge Center** that improves Time to Value (TTV) and increases product stickiness using a sequenced in-app bot and emails.
- **In-App Product Communication** that scales feedback collection across your entire user base by leveraging in-app surveys and product updates.
- A **Role-Based Landing Page** that centralizes resources and tasks for your users.
- **Email Campaigns** that efficiently increase your reach through one-to-many campaigns regarding adoption, release, and so forth.
- A **Pooled CSM Model** that manages customer accounts at scale through a distributed pooled success model.

In the Proactive phase, you might send a single email to every customer and every user: "Here's the new release. All the release notes are in the Community." However, once you enter the Personalized stage, you will want to supply each user content that is relevant to them based on the information you've gleaned about their persona and role.

In the pre-digital age, we used to alert Gainsight customers about what was coming in the next product release by posting our release notes to the

Support site. Then we would release everything. Then we would sit back and wait for support tickets to arrive so we could learn which documents were not right and where people were struggling.

Today, our process is more personalized. And we start with administrators because, often, we release features that require administrators to do something first. We send an in-app message targeting just administrators, telling them that a new feature is available, but here are the things you need to do first to get the most value from it. Four weeks later, after administrators have had time to prepare, we announce the new feature to *all* users. Then, following the release, we ask administrators to critique the timing and quality of the release.

Again, this is all done *within* the application (and sometimes by email). It is *not* done manually by a CSM. This is a prime example of how to personalize a program in a scalable way that, frankly, a CSM could never do.

Another company that has successfully entered the Personalized phase is Dealerware, a fleet management platform that launched in 2016. After the launch, the marketplace responded enthusiastically to the product, causing the company's customer base to expand from three to more than 1,000 customers in just a few years. This turbocharged growth presented a huge challenge for the Customer Success team: They needed to optimize implementation and get customers to value without having to invest major resources in additional staff. To do this, however, they needed more insight around how our customers were actually using the product.

Fortunately, Gainsight's product analytics and engagement platform provided Dealerware with the usage data they were seeking, as well as the insights necessary to improve the customer journey. The company can now drill down into users and accounts, and view specific activities and behaviors. They can see where users are getting stuck in the product (steps that are taking them longer than normal to complete) and monitor customers' interactions with the in-app engagements and training tips. Dealerware also improves adoption through timely notifications and in-app guides, and obtains direct feedback from their users via surveys.

In addition, Dealerware can segment by customer attributes and identify customers who are a good fit for potential upsells. And these upsell engagements include a call to action that connects the best prospects directly to sales, allowing them to place an order directly through the Knowledge Center bot. The sales rep can also trigger an automated follow-up email based on this interaction. All this can be accomplished within the application and with no human interaction, saving valuable time and resources internally.

"We knew we had a better chance of reaching the customer in app rather than depending on them to read a wordy email," says Morgan Redwine, Manager, Customer Success Strategy and Operations.

So we translated our best practices into interactive, targeted engagements, and our customers actually clicked through them. Our customers were responsive, and our best practices engagements had a 90 percent click-through rate. That's a 260 percent uptick in interaction when compared to when we launched these through email. We can now begin to really measure the impact of our efforts to optimize their operations. Not only did we achieve a 97 percent training interaction rate with our Getting Started section and the Knowledge Center bot, but we've attributed over $128,000 in ARR and CS upsell revenue just last year.

Our customer journey today balances just the right amount of technology and people. Now we're able to address risk and drive ROI through tools like in-app surveys and engagements. We've really been able to take our customer journey to the next level. Being able to incorporate in-app tech touch and our CS strategy has been nothing, but win-win for us.[3]

Another SaaS firm, TigerConnect, which serves hospitals and other healthcare organizations, needed a solution to improve its CS team's efficiency, reduce the number of spreadsheets and CSM notes, and scale communications and track customer health—all in one central location. In particular, CSMs were wasting a lot of time sending emails rather than focusing on the strategy sessions, training, or tactics that would move the dial.

After implementing a personalized approach to one-to-many emails, TigerConnect saw greater adoption of complex, "stickier" features, higher NPS, greater retention, and more advocacy. Just as impressive, the company increased CSM efficiency by 10 percent and reduced admin time by 20 hours per week.[4]

Obviously, the Personalization stage requires more data than the Proactive stage. Here, you need to know what users are doing in your product— what they are clicking on. You also need to know what their role is. And ideally, you also know what that person's goals are.

If the Proactive phase is about getting clients to self-serve, the Personalized phase is about sending the right person the right information at the right time, starting with an automated welcome email as soon as they've signed the contract: "We're so excited to have you as a customer! Here are three things you can do right now to start successfully using our product." (See Figure 4.4.)

On the human-led side, the pooled CSM model is an excellent strategy to adopt in this phase. Instead of assigning (say) 10 named accounts to each CSM, you put a *pool* of five CSMs in charge of managing 500 or even 1,000 accounts, with customer questions routed to different people based on their individual areas of expertise—product expertise, industry expertise, and so forth. You might also distribute the workload based on the CS activities at which each CSM excels—email campaigns for one person, training manuals for another.

Community cohorts are another strategy well suited to the Personalized phase. Cohort programs are an excellent tool for helping you develop a deeper understanding of the critical best practice needs of your customers as they progress through their journey. Instead of conducting one-to-many best practice sessions with every customer, employ a cohort-based approach during which the group walks through the key sessions in a sequenced fashion. That way, they'll not only receive the benefit of your POV but also build peer-to-peer networks that may prove immensely valuable down the road. You can further encourage such relationships by driving these users to your Community. Although this isn't a fully digital strategy, it *is* an efficient, effective, and increasingly popular way to achieve some scale. It's also a good example of how Digital + Humans = Scale.

Predictive Phase: Get Customers to Value Faster

If the Proactive phase focuses on pulling together standardized resources but leaving it to the user to figure out which resources they need, and the Personalized phase focuses on learning enough about the user to identify their goals and then guiding them to those goals, the Predictive phase focuses on forecasting what the user must do to maximize value—ASAP. Now, you are working to combine what the user wants with the value they need to quickly transform them into a loyal, higher-spend customer.

If, for example, a Gainsight customer adopts one of our products and uses it every day to manage risk, but does *not* use it to identify expansion and upsell opportunities, we know there is going to be a problem. That's because

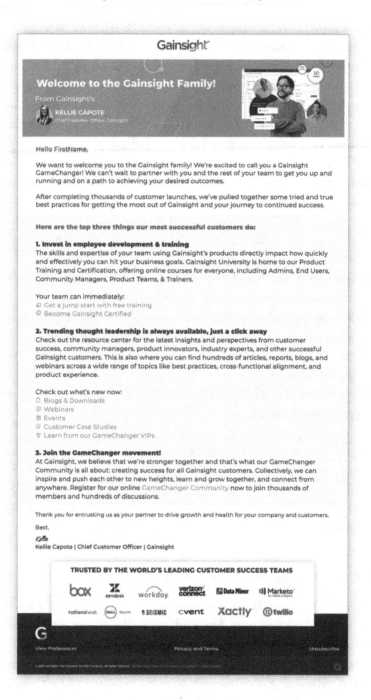

Figure 4.4   Example of a welcome email from Gainsight.

the client is overlooking a key source of value. So what we mean by *predictive* is that, once you understand what the customer's goals are, what they have purchased from you, and who the users are, you can now guide their adoption in a way that is better aligned with *their* goals (explicit and implicit) and *your* goals. You can now deliver the value they want *and* the value they need—as well as the NRR you want *and need*—faster than ever before.

In the Predictive phase, you will be employing programs that include:

- **Intelligent Journey Orchestration**, driving customers to their desired outcomes via AI-recommended user journeys. A data-driven strategy, Intelligent Journey Orchestration forecasts customer behavior across all channels to deliver, in real time, highly personalized journey recommendations.
- **In-App Content Recommendation**, accelerating users toward value realization through in-app recommendations.
- **Single Digital Destination** that seamlessly connect your customers with Community, product, and your teams—for example, a landing page customer hub that provides a centralized and more integrated digital experience.
- **Multichannel Analytics** that measure the impact and attribution of your digital campaigns.

When cybersecurity firm RiskIQ wanted to scale its CS operation, it implemented a Journey Orchestration strategy to reduce the cost of customer-facing activities and translated its manual customer health index into an automated health scorecard, increasing its NRR to more than 100 percent.[5]

You Can Occupy Multiple Levels of Maturity

It is likely that some of the techniques and tools you will use in the Predictive phase will have first been deployed during the Reactive phase. At Gainsight, for example, we have long looked for early-warning signals that a customer is in danger of churning. However, by the time we reach the Proactive phase, our goal is not only to prevent churn through well-crafted interventions but to proactively locate expansion opportunities as well.

By the time we enter the Personalized phase, we are better at locating expansion and upsell opportunities, thanks to what we now know about users; by the Predictive phase, we can accurately forecast what we and our customers must do—from the start of the relationship—to optimize TTV.

So, much as we humans acquire skills and learnings as we progress from childhood to maturity, your company and CS organization will acquire—and build upon—different digital skills, resources, and best practices as you move from the Reactive to the Predictive stages of the Digital CS maturity model. This *is* a linear progression, but you can (and probably will) occupy multiple levels of maturity at any given time. In other words, as you move forward, your arsenal of Digital CS systems, processes, and motions will reflect different stages of maturity.

For example, maybe your self-service processes harken back to your arrival at the Proactive stage, while your onboarding tools and design are more personalized. At the same time, maybe you haven't yet applied automation to the renewal process or to increasing adoption rates. This is normal.

As you move forward, we recommend that you and your team continuously review the customer journey to determine, from an efficiency standpoint, what your customers are currently doing versus what they *should* be doing. From there, you can determine which digital strategies and use cases are best suited to solving problems. You might say, "I think we need to be more proactive with onboarding. How can we improve our processes, using digital, to enhance efficiency? What are the first steps we can take, and which human, technological, and financial resources will we need to take these steps and realize these improvements?"

To that end, in the next three chapters, we recommend several different methods that you can use to get started in each maturity phase. The idea here is that you might start with a personalized solution to improve one aspect of the customer journey while applying a Proactive solution to another aspect. For example, you might decide to send welcome emails targeted by user role to help with onboarding—a use case from the Personalization stage—even as you continue to refine Proactive processes and systems. Those welcome emails are a great way to dip your toes into the personalized waters—even if you haven't yet mastered all the swimming strokes, styles, and techniques of the Proactive stage.

Okta's Journey to Digital Maturity

About four years ago, when Melissa Allen joined Okta as Senior Manager of Customer Success Operations, 80 percent of the customers had no CSM coverage or digital touchpoints. Recognizing the untapped opportunity this presented, Allen spearheaded the launch of the company's first Digital CS initiative.

Says Allen:

> We started with simple email programs, and have really expanded since then. In the beginning, we were just trying to reach out to non-CSM covered accounts, but we soon realized that digital CS shouldn't be a segment. It needs to be a strategy—one where we provide every segment of customer with the same awesome digital experience while also supporting the CSMs, having the digital journey serve as a supplement to what they're already adding.
>
> Today, we have very focused, customized emails for adoption, along with a pooled human touch at the end of certain programs to aid with increased adoption. We also do in-app messaging, which we sometimes utilize in tandem with the email programs. At other times, the focus is solely in app. These programs let us utilize the user role of the individual to customize messages. If you're an admin, it prompts you for that. If you're a regular user, depending on your permission sets, you can customize the messaging so it's relevant to you, not just generic.
>
> More recently, we deployed a customized video to customers. We email customers with this dynamic video. Once it's opened, it pulls in data and is able to run a beautiful automated video that is super-customized to the user receiving it. We've also created a collaborative success hub, where we store QBRs, NVRs, and one-pagers such as our business value report. Customers can log in at any time and access it, and the CSMs can add to it. Our digital growth team can mass-create one-pagers and save them there. This has been a huge success. Last quarter, we had over 10,000 views in our success hub of the one-pagers and QBRs.

Okta's Digital Growth team is the primary driver of Digital CS. They decide on content, paths, and personas, but the Operations team works with Digital Growth as well as with the data team and business systems team to determine which data points can be integrated into Salesforce or Gainsight to help create highly customized digital programs.

After we feed that data into Salesforce or Gainsight, those programs can say to customers, "We noticed you turned on *this* feature. Amazing. What about *that* feature?" We now have data to tell us that users activated feature X, but not feature Y, so let's send them a customized email about their actions to help them keep adopting.

We also have a content team that helps make sure we're aligned with Okta's overall messaging. And marketing gets involved for the branding side of it. We don't have marketing working on the automated emails, but we make sure those emails are aligned with Okta's branding. We want all our messaging to look like it's coming from the same company.

Another thing we do is have CS operations build out a quarterly Gainsight roadmap. We meet with this team every two weeks to make sure we're prioritizing the right things and to ensure that the collaborations between all the different teams are on track. In other words, Digital CS is not about a handful of folks in CS doing digital growth. This is a company-wide initiative.

How did Allen go about scaling the digital programs?

Initially, you need to take a step back and look at what your focuses are. We wanted to provide a seamless onboarding experience. We wanted customers to adopt the products they purchased. We wanted them to see the value in what they purchased. So we took these focuses and we said, "How do we create KPIs around these things?"

To scale customization and automation, we used templates that have different variants based on customizable features. Suddenly, we only had to develop one digital program. Previously, we would've needed 20 programs to achieve what we can now do with just one. It allows us so much variability and so much customization, and that *does* help with scaling, as does the automation of triggers—either event-based triggers or time-based triggers. Once you build a campaign, you step back and watch the results, and then decide if you need to go back and iterate.

As for metrics, we look at how many digital engagements we've had within certain timeframes. We're asking, "How many digital engagements did we have in the past quarter? What about the last fiscal year? What about fiscal year over year?" Then we determine if we need to iterate or even start over. Maybe something's not doing what it used to, so maybe we pull that out and we put something else in. It allows us to really analyze and pivot if we need to.

What we've learned, so far, is that the customers who engage—who actually open the emails—have a higher renewal rate, a higher health score, and a higher activation and adoption rate than those who don't open the emails. The exciting part is that we're just getting started. There's so much more data to pull, so many more things that we can grab to create a customized journey. Today, we're sending extremely relevant messaging. And obviously, the more relevant the message, the higher the open rate, the better they're going to adopt.

Moving forward, we want to explore more with video messaging. Video really draws people in. I feel like we've just scratched the surface with video, and—of course—we're also interested in learning how we can leverage AI. We're just starting to explore the possibilities.[6]

"Perfect Is the Enemy of Good"

Digital success can become very complex, very fast. (We are a leading company in this field, and it can sometimes feel very complex to us!) That said, there's no reason you can't get started—and started quickly—with a few simple steps. Reaching full digital maturity—the point at which everything is predictive—is going to take years, depending on how fast technology, especially AI, continues to advance. In the meantime, don't get stuck. Don't get bogged down worrying whether all your data is correct or whether you've set up the perfect customer journey.

Keeping in mind that "perfect is the enemy of good," we will show you plenty of ways to quickly get started in the chapters ahead. For example, you could set up and launch an in-app knowledge bot in about a week, which will provide a more efficient and enjoyable onboarding experience for you and your users. The same goes for launching an enhanced customer hub. Even as you take baby steps within the Proactive realm, you can be thinking ahead about ways to transform your Community into a more personalized portal. You can be designing a digital destination that recommends what customers should be doing next based on their user roles.

At the very least, you can get started by sending more personalized emails. Of course, this does require a little bit of data (user types), but once you collect that data, you can start running email campaigns that will increase engagement by speaking directly, and personally, to every end user. In fact, you can use digital strategies to start refining your current data and acquiring more data—for example, by using in-app engagements to confirm contact information, user roles, and the like.

No longer will people glance at your emails and think, "Ugh! This isn't relevant! Why do they keep sending me this generic spam?" Personalized email campaigns are something you could be doing right now. There's no reason to wait, and there are plenty of reasons to embark on this leg of your Digital CS journey today.

Summary

Most SaaS companies are dipping their toes into digital waters, but many have not yet learned how to swim. Although they now have access to digital CS resources, they have not yet entered the realm of true Digital CS. In this Reactive phase, CS typically responds to customer needs only *after* the customer verbalizes those needs, in an improvised fashion, and with resources that are unorganized and siloed. This produces inefficiencies and a poor customer experience.

Based on customer conversations and industry analysis, we've developed a model to help SaaS companies identify, understand, and progress through the stages of Digital CS Maturity, which we've labeled the Proactive, Personalized, and Predictive stages.

In the Proactive stage of Digital CS maturity, your mission is to empower users to self-serve with centralized resources and guides.

In the Personalized phase of Digital CS, your goal is to enable distinct user journeys, automated by data, that influence successful customer behaviors. These journeys are orchestrated by data-driven, scalable, one-to-many programs that are integrated within (and around) the product.

The Predictive stage is the apex of Digital Customer Success. By this point in your maturity, you are designing intelligent customer experiences, powered by omnichannel technologies, that *very quickly* drive customers to their desired business outcomes.

As you move forward, we recommend that you and your team continually review the customer journey to determine, from an efficiency standpoint, what customers are currently doing versus what they *should* be doing. From there, you can determine which digital strategies and use cases are best suited to solving any problems.

5

Launching the Proactive Phase of Your Digital CS Program

Proactive Phase	
Strategy:	**Customer Self-Service**
Key Use Cases:	Self-Service Enablement
	One-to-Many Customer Communications
	Digital-Led Onboarding
Tactics:	Link to Central Resources
	Simple Email Campaigns
	In-App Checklist

The hardest part of launching a Digital CS program is figuring out where to begin. We see this every day at Gainsight. Time and again, working with customers to help them develop their digital programs, we receive pushback, such as "I *want* to develop more personalized email campaigns, but I don't trust my contact data" or "If I'm going to go digital, I first need to break out the whiteboard and map every single journey and every permutation of the program, so I'm not ready to start." Underlying this pushback is the sort of "analysis paralysis" that stems from overcomplicating the challenges and/or thinking that you need to accomplish everything at once.

Our advice?

Stop overthinking the challenges and opportunities in front of you, and don't try to accelerate from zero to 100 overnight. Instead, pick a logical starting point for your Digital CS program—one based on a customer challenge that's relatively easy to solve using one or more of the use cases and channels just cited. As Calvin Coolidge once said, "We cannot do everything at once, but we can do *something* at once." So instead of worrying about the latest CSAT scores or fretting over last year's churn rates, do *something* now. Launch your organization into the Proactive phase of Digital Success.

In this first phase of digital maturity, your main goals are to boost customer retention and satisfaction, and accelerate Time to Value (TTV) by improving user onboarding processes, boosting product adoption rates, and giving users the ability to find the answers to their questions on their own—without having to contact Support or a CSM. And you do this by empowering users to self-serve with centralized resources and guides.

With this in mind, the first step on your Digital Success journey is to choose a specific customer challenge that you want to solve, along with the tool(s) best suited for resolving it.

Self-Service Enablement

If the most immediate challenge that you want to address is providing your customers with an integrated way to self-serve and educate themselves about your products or services, Self-Service Enablement is a use case you should pursue. Here's how we would outline our approach to this use case:

Challenge:

Our teams are constantly fielding the same questions over and over. Providing one-to-one support for the same sets of questions is not an efficient use of our team's time and is limiting our ability to scale.

Worse, we are sometimes unable to help customers find immediate answers to their needs, thus increasing the costs of serving each customer. Customers are also frustrated with the inefficiencies associated with having to reach out and wait for a response, especially when no quick solution to their problem is forthcoming.

Solution:

A simple, self-serve way for customers to find answers within a centralized digital resource center. This will surface the answers that users want, providing them with real-time support and quick access to peer-to-peer education via our Community.

Important Personas:

- Post-Sales Leader and CS Leader
- CS Ops Leader
- CSM and Support Managers
- Community Manager
- Education Services Leader
- Product Manager

Before Scenario:

- Customer-facing teams spend most of their day responding to the same questions over and over.
- Customers cannot find answers on their own, so they need to turn to manual human support for everything.
- Customers must look in multiple, disparate places for resources that answer their questions.

After Scenario:

- Teams see an increase in support ticket deflection, ultimately reducing their workload and the associated costs.
- Customers can self-serve and increase engagement through Community and P2P resources.
- Internal teams can use their time more efficiently to prioritize higher-value activities for customers.

Four Steps to Better Self Service

How can you establish—or improve—self-service in your own organization? Here are four steps that will help you deliver remarkable self-service and next-level user engagement:

1. **Tap the expertise in your community.** For most B2B SaaS companies, speaking to customers traditionally involved webinars, meetups, and in-person events. Roundtables were a mainstay when it came to gathering customer information on your product and service. This is where online user communities have changed the game. Who better to offer advice and respond to queries about your product than the customers who actually use it every day?

   Online communities give users a transparent platform to interact and share best practices with each other—and you. In addition, your Customer Success team can easily make announcements in the community, ensuring that users are continually updated with any product changes or new features. This decreases the likelihood that users will need to get in touch with your team directly.

   Allowing customers to vote on the best answers in a Community also increases interaction and reduces pressure on your Customer Support teams by enabling users to self-serve and help each other. What's more, online communities foster the feeling among customers that they are part of an interesting, interactive group, and this in itself drives engagement. (To boost competitiveness and camaraderie among members, some SaaS companies are using gamification to award superusers customized badges.) Most important, harnessing the power of your user Community can deflect 25 to 50 percent of the support tickets currently hitting your team.

2. **Provide an online knowledge base.** The ultimate way to make the most of self-service is to collect all the content created within your online Community and use it to fuel a knowledge base or customer hub—the one-stop content shop where your customers can immediately access resources such as blogs, thought-leadership articles, product announcements, onboarding information, best-practice videos, and training webinars.

3. **Make your CS content easily accessible.** It should go without saying that making your content easily accessible is key to successful self-service. If customers can't find the content they're seeking, it may as well not be there at all. But with a dynamic online Community + Knowledge Base combination, you can quickly and easily distribute great CS content—from how-to material and case studies to tips, tricks, and tutorials—across your entire customer community. Using an in-app knowledge center bot, you can even embed content directly within the product experience and promote (or simplify) access to the Community and customer hub.

   Although Community may serve as the entry point for users looking to self-serve, it's important to support users at all stages of the customer journey. Therefore, be sure that your users can obtain instant and highly relevant content no matter where they are within your product or website. Don't make customers search long and hard for the help they need. Deliver it proactively with in-product, in-app, and in-site embeddable widgets supported by a federated search capability. In addition, you may want to use APIs to inject posts, knowledge articles, and support docs wherever your users may need them.

4. **Make sure a human CSM or Support rep is *always* within easy reach.** Remember: Digital CS is designed to supplement—not replace—human-led Customer Success and Customer Support. For that reason, *always* give your users a lightning-fast method for reaching a human being whenever they need to speak with one. Always!

Although B2C companies can sometimes get away with inadvertently herding customers into "automated doom loops"—in which customers are unable to reach a human support rep no matter how many buttons they press—B2B organizations cannot afford to alienate paying customers in this way. Although many B2B customers are eager to use a self-service IVR option for quick questions and easy-to-handle tasks, many will (understandably) want to chat with a live support person for complex, high-value interactions.

Just because your customers can self-serve doesn't mean that you should stop interacting with them completely. In fact, staying in touch with users is one of the best ways to drive happiness and retention, no matter how good your self-service offerings are. That's why it's crucial to ensure that your Customer Support and/or Success teams are ready to assist when other product users or Community managers can't help.

As one McKinsey report neatly put it, "The trick is striking the right balance between digital and human interaction in B2B's more complex customer relationships."[1]

Unqork Uncorks the Power of a Customer Hub

Unqork, the leading codeless as a service platform, recently teamed with Gainsight to upgrade its user Community into a more powerful, more appealing digital destination that could accelerate product adoption and customer TTV through expanded content offerings and enhanced P2P support. Although the initiative is still relatively young, Unqork's customer hub is increasingly popular with users and increasingly efficient from a CS standpoint.

Danny Pancratz, Director of Community at Unqork, explained:

> The challenge we were looking to solve came directly from our customers. They told us they had a lot of great resources that we had created [but the resources were scattered across different locations]. They told us, "You have all these great things, but my experience with you is pretty bad. I have 10-plus bookmarks of resources for your platform." They asked us for a better experience, and customer hub became our solution, because it is really aligned with giving our customers what they were asking for.

One year into the Community upgrade, the number of answers provided by external users rose from 22 percent to more than 80 percent. This has reduced the time demands on internal experts, allowing them to shift their focus to higher-impact questions that only they can answer. At the same time, Unqork improved the answer rate of questions by nearly 30 percent and achieved reply rates close to 100 percent.

In addition, the company began introducing a variety of live and digital content on the platform—all designed to increase user engagement while decreasing the amount of time that post-sales staff must dedicate to keeping customers updated and informed. For example, the company now posts a series of short-form videos to the Community, each covering a single topic. To date, this micro-content strategy has proven so successful that it has been extended to staff-produced webinars and twitch livestreams, making content easier to find and consume. Seventy-five percent of speakers have been non-staff Community members, livestream attendance is solid, and hundreds of hours of videos have been watched at later times.

Shortly after the launch of the video series, Unqork also began publishing a blog on the Community to increase customer awareness of new resources and important updates on how to use features. (Previously, such documentation was accessible only on another platform.) Today, "release notes" for documentation are published once or twice a month in a blog. Most blog posts receive 250 to 300 views apiece, and overall, the Community has become the #3 source of traffic to Unqork's documentation, behind only direct traffic and Google searches.

Finally, to make it easier to access the Community's customer hub features without the friction of logging in, Unqork product updates, digital events, and other content is now visible and indexable for search, and the navigation menu can "show" users the Community even if they don't log in. This has resulted in a 160 percent increase in monthly user traffic.

Said Pancratz:

> When it comes to managing cross-functional alignment, the most important thing is helping our customers. So aligning with that is number one, and then unpacking all the different ways they need help. It's about creating a cohesive customer hub, a Community hub experience. A great lesson I learned from the CMO at a previous job was that the customer shouldn't see your org chart. And that's what was happening for us. It takes a lot of people, and there are a lot of problems that we need to solve for our customers, as well as ways to help them be successful, that are owned by different parts of our business. But that's not necessarily the experience we want to show customers: Go here for this and go there for that. So cross-functional alignment on the customer hub experience enables us to make it easy for the customer—easy to connect them to the people and resources they need to be successful.
>
> Connection is what powers our Community. And in terms of Digital Customer Success, the Community allows us to make the things that need to be immediate, really easy and fast as a launch pad for Customer Success. And what this self-service also does is allow our CSMs, our

support team, and experts from Product and other parts of the business to have a higher impact when they're connecting directly.

The thing that I like best about the customer hub is the tools that allow me to customize the experience and bring the things that are unique about our Community to light, and also the extensibility. So between customization and extensibility, I'm usually able to turn every idea I have for the Community into reality. There are a lot of great things I do with automation that allow me to not just survive as a Community manager and team of one, but also to thrive. The most important aspect of that is when you can turn ideas or pain points you hear from your Community members into solutions that improve your Community. That's where you can really create new value for your customers, which is what it's all about.[2]

If you aren't sure whether to start with a customer hub or a simple Community, consider what type of company you are. For example, if you're a Product-Led Growth (PLG) company, Community is probably the best option because your individual users are already training themselves to use the product and expand their use of it. In other words, they're already accustomed to self-serving. By adding a Community, you can accelerate their TTV by directing them to a place where they can learn from one another and share best practices.

If, in contrast, your company has historically relied on human-led Customer Success and Support, a customer hub would probably make more sense—at least as a starting point. This solution is better suited to users who aren't accustomed to self-service—users who tend to want educational resources that are more basic and comprehensive.

One-to-Many Customer Communications

If the first challenge you want to address is reaching your customers via digital touchpoints to encourage adoption, assess sentiment, and build deeper relationships, one-to-many customer communications is an ideal use case for digital technologies.

Challenge:

Our customers are often hard to reach, requiring multiple attempts from customer-facing teams to get in touch. Customers are also only using a few features regularly and not deeply engaging with what our product is capable of doing, resulting in churn.

Solution:

A centralized, curated way to reach customers with one-to-many content that uses digital engagements in product and encourages them to fully adopt features while building deeper, more meaningful communities.

Important Personas:

- Post-Sales Leader and CS Leader
- CS Ops Leader
- CSM and Support Managers
- Community Manager
- Product Manager

Before Scenario:

- Customers are nonresponsive to emails and calls from our customer-facing teams, and their sentiment is unknown.
- Customers are only scratching the surface of our capabilities and never going beyond basic usage.
- Customers aren't aware of, or engaging with, our current one-to-many programs, and instead they ask repeated questions.

After Scenario:

- Teams get improved engagement from customers on usage and sentiment scoring.
- Customers are more likely to renew as their engagement and usage broadens via Community and in-app content.
- Internal teams can use their time more efficiently and eliminate continuous outreach tasks.

One-to-many customer communications is a multichannel use case that can involve emails, webinars, videos, social media, surveys, and more. However, if you are not yet ready to guide customers to a centralized destination—your community or customer hub—where they can access these communications, ask deeper questions, read about best practices, and uplevel their product usage, a good way to launch your digital one-to-many communications program is with an enhanced email campaign—"enhanced" in the sense that (at a minimum) it will be slightly more targeted and slightly more personalized than a generic email campaign.

Figure 5.1 shows an example of a one-to-many customer communication via email.

You Don't Build a Relationship with an Inbox

Some of you may be thinking "We already have targeted, one-to-many customer communications," while others of you may be saying "We would love to do this, but how do we start? We don't have internal alignment on who talks to the customer, and I'm not sure we have the necessary data for communicating with the right people at the right time."

If you're in the latter camp, our advice is this: Generic emails no longer work, so start taking baby steps to deliver more targeted, and more personalized, messages.

You don't need to know much about your users to provide them with targeted messaging that's a notch above the generic "Hi, User. We just released this new feature. Come check it out." All you need to know is with whom you are talking (the user's role) and what information they need to have.

This is a recommendation that often elicits *a lot* of pushback from customers who are just embarking on their Digital Success journey: "I *want* to do this, but I don't trust my data. I need to get my data in order. I need to figure out the contact information." In response, we usually reply with: "There are tools that can help you collect the user data you need. At the very least, send a survey to all your contacts that says, "If you tell us a little more about who you are, we can customize your experience." Collecting this user data will not only enable your first one-to-many communications campaign of the Proactive stage; it can also help you to start laying the foundations for your entry into the second phase of Digital CS maturity—the Personalized Phase (see Chapter 6).

At Alteryx, the leading analytics automation platform (and a winner of Gainsight's 2023 GameChanger award), one-to-many emails are a primary engagement methodology. Alteryx's longest-standing program is its End User Onboarding, which has delivered communications to over 50,000 end users across more than 3,000 accounts since its release in July 2022.

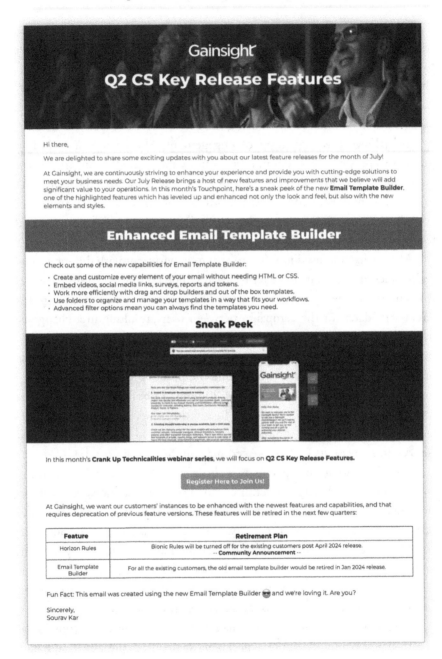

Figure 5.1   Example of one-to-many customer communication from Gainsight.

Using Gainsight's Journey Orchestrator (JO), an automated email feature that enables admins to design email templates and schedule programs to reach the right customers at the right time, Alteryx sends a "welcome-aboard" communication whenever a new user activates. This timely communication generated an industry-leading 35 percent open rate and a 30 percent click-through rate during the first quarter of fiscal year 2023.

To achieve this high level of engagement, Alteryx uses a Gainsight product to personalize its communications by including the customer's first name and the CSM's name in the message. They also use the platform's HTML capabilities to add a CSM headshot within their emails and other communications. This helps to form a stronger connection with the end user—a connection that comes across as both authentic and personal.

Alteryx has also used its CS platform to experiment with different messaging and email layouts in order to learn which communications packages generate the highest engagement rates. The company even tested with different start dates for the campaign between users, resulting in a change of the delivery time for communications from Day 1 to Day 4 following activation. (The change was made after learning that, while many users activate immediately, they often don't start using the product for several days.)

This workflow once took a CSM 20 hours to build. Today, it takes just one hour to integrate a new product. In addition, the company now collects feedback that helps it optimize where CSMs spend their time, allowing Alteryx to increase its CSM-to-Account ratio from 1:30 to a 1:120![3]

Launching email campaigns like those used by Alteryx is something you can do immediately. Something you should *not* do, however, is flood customers with too many emails. "All right! We now have a one-to-many customer communications capability. Let's start nudging our customers to do A, B, and C by sending them one email after another until they respond in the way we want." (Frankly, the only thing worse than a generic email is a relentless barrage of slightly more targeted, slightly more personalized emails that your customers will regard as irritating spam.)

Deciding whether to employ email or another channel for your initial one-to-many communications will largely depend on the target audience you want to reach. For example: If the target audience comprises end users, you will likely generate more engagement by using in-app communications, because this is where most end users live. (We use an in-app engagement/walkthrough whenever a new user logs in to Gainsight for the first time.)

By contrast, if the target audience comprises executives who rarely log in to the product, crafting an in-app message is a waste of time. (You may as well lease billboards on the ocean floor. The resulting engagement will probably be the same.)

Think about whom you're talking to, what you need them to do, and which channel or technological capabilities you could leverage to resolve the customer's challenge, as well as your own challenges. At the Proactive stage, one of your key goals is doing more with less. Toward that end, one-to-many communications are an excellent way to boost the efficiency and performance of your CS team.

Consider all the information that a customer typically needs, which is currently communicated manually by your CSMs in the form of repetitive emails. Consider how much time your CSMs spend on these tasks every day. Then consider how much time your CSMs will save after you automate parts of this process and where else they could spend that time.

Consider, also, how much more *effective* your one-to-many communications could be by making them just a little more targeted and personalized.

As an example, let's look at feature adoption. Here at Gainsight, our release program has a quarterly frequency. Every quarter, there is a new feature release communication that might contain information about (say) 50 different features. In reality, 10 of the features might be of interest to every customer, while the remaining 40 were "little goodies" designed for specific subsegments of our customer base. In the past, we would direct one-to-many communications to the Ops teams of our customers (and maybe the executives). Unfortunately, these messages didn't always "speak" to either audience. As a result, our CSMs sometimes had to call (or arrange meetings with) key personas to convince them that features x, y and z were "exactly what you are looking for. Please start using them."

Today, we have largely liberated our CSMs from this kind of tedious work by customizing our messages and directing them to particular audiences and personas within our customers' organizations. For example (as we mentioned in the last chapter), we often start by sending a special release email to only the administrators—a note that says something like "Here's what's coming up, and here's what you need to do to get ready." Only *after* this communication is sent do we follow up a little later by sending customized emails to all the end users to get them excited about the business value they can realize from the new features. This encourages the business team to approach the Ops team and say, "We just learned about this new feature. How do we get started?"

From a communications perspective, what we are doing is appealing directly to each of these different users in a way that makes sense to each of them. We are speaking in each user's particular "language," getting them excited about the value that they themselves will obtain from adopting the new feature(s).

In the past, a CSM would have to schedule individual meetings with different stakeholders, convince them to get in a room together, hope that they agreed on how to move forward, and then hope that they actually *did* move forward.

But after implementing your new one-to-many communications program around new product/feature releases, you change the dynamics from push to pull. Now it's the administrator who reaches out to your CSM and says, "Hey, I saw this feature. My boss is excited about it. Let's talk about how we roll it out to the company."

Today, this is how we think about adoption journeys. We use a playbook borrowed from Marketing: We generate awareness; we get different audiences excited about new offerings; we ensure that everyone knows how to move forward (by including in-app training guides, etc.); and, finally, we solicit feedback to help us improve the process for the next adoption journey.

Digital-Led Onboarding

Want a scalable way to accelerate TTV by providing digital user guidance and training (and removing friction) during the onboarding experience? Onboarding is a particularly crucial moment in the customer life cycle. It is your opportunity to make a great (or poor) first impression on the customer, setting the tone and direction of the entire relationship.

Often there is a clear correlation between churn and a poor onboarding experience—one in which users "fail to launch" or limit themselves to only basic product features. Digital-led onboarding can ensure that you put your best foot forward in a very scalable way.

Challenge:

Customers rely on customer-facing teams to onboard and train them. This frequently causes delays in product activation and adoption as well as slow TTV. When scaling, teams are hard pressed to onboard new customers in a timely way with manual, unscalable processes.

Solution:

A programmatic digital approach to onboarding that leverages prescriptive journey automation to quickly guide users to value—in-product and via Community programs.

Important Personas:

- Post-Sales Leader and CS Leader
- CS Ops Leader
- CSM and Support Managers
- Community Manager
- Education Services Leader
- Product Manager

Before Scenario:

- Customer-facing teams often encounter scheduling delays in getting users manually onboarded as well as time-intensive training.
- Customers miss activation of key features, resulting in low adoption and ROI from products.
- Scale is impossible with highly manual programs and large numbers of new users.

After Scenario:

- Curated onboarding experiences ensure that high-value features are activated and adopted, resulting in improved TTV.
- Customer-facing teams save hours of manual outreach and training time onboarding new users.
- Account ratios can be maximized while still ensuring that key milestones are reached in a customer's onboarding journey.

Think of the positive impact that a Digital-led onboarding program could have on an individual CSM, especially one charged with serving enterprise clients—clients that spend six- or seven-figure sums for an annual subscription, each of which has dozens or hundreds of users joining and leaving the company every year. In any given month, your CSM may be tasked with onboarding 50 (or more) new users per customer—practically a full-time job in itself. The reality, therefore, is that many users are not properly onboarded in a solely CSM-led way because CSMs can work with only a few key stakeholders (e.g., the admin, Ops leader, sponsor, etc.). Without Digital-led onboarding, you're missing an opportunity to drive a better onboarding experience for all your users.

Stress. Fatigue. Burnout. These are all occupational hazards of CSMs whose plates are piled high with competing priorities and recurring activities, especially when those activities—like onboarding—are both repetitive and a high priority. Digital-led programs can even allow you to automate the entire onboarding process. Or, in cases where your product requires professional services engagements, Digital-led programs offer you an opportunity to augment manual training with digital, which can help enhance the user experience, learning management, and the like.

Unlike many of the CSM workloads that digital programs are designed to lighten, onboarding is *not* a low-value activity. In this case, Digital CS can assist your CSMs in executing the high-value motions needed to accelerate onboarding, adoption, and TTV.

By using a CS technology platform, your CSM can instantly detect when a new user logs in to your product. From there, the platform automatically sends that new user an onboarding checklist: "We've never seen you before. Here are the top three things you should do when you log into our platform: (1) confirm your email address; (2) set up your notifications; and (3) perform your first action—e.g., write your first note about a customer." (You could also make the program available in product—via onboarding guides and a Knowledge Center bot.)

Without a Digital-Led Onboarding program, your CSM would have to manually welcome new users to the product and facilitate every training session. Yes, the CSM would be focused on providing a high-value service, but they would also be devoting a lot of time to a tedious process that digital technology can perform without becoming bored or burned out. Just imagine what your CSM could accomplish if they didn't have to set aside hours and hours of time every month to monitor and train all those new users! At the very least, they could devote several more hours per week to identifying—and acting on—churn risk, expansion, upsell, and advocacy opportunities among the various personas within each customer.

For the customer, a superior Digital CE program such as onboarding should provide a seamless experience. The content should be searchable, easy to find, easy to access, and have a uniform look, feel, and flow—even when the customer is transitioning from asset to asset or platform to platform. In other words, everything should be intertwined. Every message should appear to be part of the same cohesive journey delivered by the same brand.

As you ponder how to deliver a superior onboarding, adoption, or other CE experience, look for ways to inspire the customer to adopt your product and features in new and more sophisticated ways. Think of how you can inspire them at every point in the journey by showing them the art of the possible. At the same time, whenever there's a point of friction or resistance, make sure users are able to overcome it in as few steps as possible.

Ideally, onboarding (and other CE) programs will become so embedded in the overall customer experience that users won't always recognize that they're *having* an educational experience—something separate and distinct from the product experience. Instead, the educational experience will organically mesh with the user's desire to get more value from the product—just as your experience watching a DIY YouTube video meshes with your desire to fix a leaky faucet or replace a broken toilet.

Digital-Led Onboarding: Best Practices from Samsara

At Samsara, the pioneer of the Connected Operations Cloud and another Gainsight GameChanger award winner, Digital-Led Onboarding enables the CS team to onboard and engage with customers at scale, allowing them to prioritize their time on risk intervention and other high-value engagements. The goals: Decrease their customers' time to value and increase ROI and NRR.

During the first customer lifecycle stage of onboarding a Samsara Implementation Consultant is dedicated to getting the customer trained and implemented on the Samsara system. The goal is for customers to quickly see value and feel educated on how to use their dashboard/products.

After the sale, the team uses a hand-off engagement between Sales and Customer Success to pass the relationship from the pre-sales teams to the post-sales team and to help customers understand what will happen next.

Within this hand-off email, there is a link to an onboarding checklist to help the customer prepare for the onboarding process and understand what success looks like. Forwarding this checklist at the time of purchase is designed to prevent any delays in onboarding progress.

Week 1 | Onboarding Checklist

Welcome to your first week of onboarding! There are many simple - but meaningful - steps you should take this week to prepare your team for a successful transition to the product. Complete each of the steps below to stay on track and make the most out of your investment.

BEFORE YOU BEGIN

☐ Create Your Dashboard .... 5 Minute Task

☐ Attend One of the Weekly "Getting Started" Webinars .... 1 Hr. Task

1. PREPARE FOR YOUR INSTALLATION

☐ Product Activation .... 5 Minute Task

☐ Download the Samsara Fleet App .... 3 Minute Task

☐ Create Implementation Plan .... 20 Minute Task

2. CONFIGURE YOUR BASIC SETTINGS

☐ Take the eLearning Course - Settings .... 30 Minute. Task

☐ Configure Your Settings .... 3 Minute Task

    ☐ Customize Your Organization Name

    ☐ Add Your Company Logo

    ☐ Set Defaults

☐ Create Your Dashboard User Profiles .... 5 Minute Task

☐ Create Your Driver User Profiles .... 5 Minute Task

☐ Configure Your Basic Settings .... 12 Minute Task

☐ Complete compliance requirements .... 9 Minute Task

    ☐ Add Your Name, Main Office Address, & Regulatory Number | *Dive Deeper*

    ☐ Configure Compliance Rulesets | *Dive Deeper*

Ready for Week 2? Check it out *here*

Figure 5.2 Example of an onboarding checklist.

On Day 1 of onboarding, a welcome email is generated to welcome the customer to the Customer Success team and outline the steps they need to be successful during onboarding. The goal of this email is to decrease the time-to-value for each customer and get them up and running quickly.

From there, customer communications can take many forms, including text messages, emails, and in-dashboard pop-ups. These communications include progress updates, helpful reminders and best practices, and tips on how to successfully onboard with Samsara. Over the next few weeks of the onboarding period, an onboarding progress update is sent on a weekly basis. These progress update emails inform the customer of their progress against their onboarding goals and persuade customers to install quickly and engage with the company's many forms of training content (including its Academy and Live New User webinars).

About halfway through onboarding, if the customer is failing to onboard, the Samsara Implementation team provides more hands-on support to get them up and running as soon as possible.

At the same time, customers who have successfully onboarded receive an Onboarding Success email, which congratulates them for having completed the appropriate onboarding steps and reminds them of the resources that are available to them moving forward. The goal of this email is to recognize successful onboarding and ensure that the customer has access to all available self-service tools.

On the last day of the onboarding window, customers are sent an onboarding close-out email informing them that their 30-day onboarding assistance window has ended. The email also provides them with all applicable self-service tools and resources moving forward.

The last step within the onboarding journey is to send an Onboarding CSAT survey, which is intended to help the CS team better understand the customer's experience throughout the onboarding period and where they might need to improve. Depending on if the customer submits a high or low score, they will be sent down a different journey, either encouraging customers to become advocates or giving customers the opportunity to speak with an Implementation team member again.

Throughout the entirety of their relationship with Samsara, customers are encouraged to fuse the Samsara Academy, a customer-facing learning management system, via the client dashboard. The Samsara Academy is designed to provide custom training modules for each customer based on the products they purchased and the role they have. The goal of this self-service tool is to decrease TTV for each customer and get them up and running quickly.

In addition, at the start of the Samsara subscription, registration links are emailed to customers to Live New User webinars. These onboarding webinars aim to provide a more personalized and engaging training experience for customers. (The webinars even include a Q&A component to address client questions directly.) The goal of the webinar is to decrease TTV for each customer and get them up and running quickly.

Ongoing Education and Engagement

Samsara's efforts to engage with, and continue to train and educate its customers, do not stop at the conclusion of the official onboarding period. Not by a long shot. Instead, the company uses a variety of programs and channels to ensure that customers achieve their desired outcomes and value as soon as possible. These programs include:

- **Product Adoption Campaigns:** Digital multi-email campaigns that are specific to a customer's key value points or reason for purchasing. The emails encourage customers to set goals and attend webinars on topics related to their product areas.
- **Ongoing Education:** In addition to webinars, Samsara promotes Samsara Academy Spotlights (via emails sent during the second week of each month) that highlight one or two new or relevant training videos. The goal of these emails is to increase adoption with Samsara Academy and help customers stay current with important product updates and changes.
- **NPS Surveys:** These are sent out every 90 days.

Milestone celebration emails are linked to specific customer achievements such as the completion of onboarding or when a particular goal is achieved (e.g., when the customer improves their safety score).

Summary

The hardest part of launching a Digital CS program is figuring out where to begin. Our advice is to pick a customer challenge that's relatively easy to solve using one or more of the self-service use cases and channels recommended in this chapter.

If the most immediate challenge you wish to address is providing customers with an integrated way to self-serve and educate themselves about your products, design a simple, self-serve way for customers to find answers within a centralized digital resource center. This customer hub will surface the answers that users want, providing them with real-time support and quick access to peer-to-peer education via the Community. Additional benefits include an increase in support ticket deflection, heightened customer engagement via Community, and greater efficiency of internal teams, who can now focus on higher-value activities.

If the first challenge you want to address is reaching your customers via digital touchpoints to encourage adoption, assess sentiment, and build deeper relationships, One-to-Many Customer Communications is an ideal use case. A centralized, curated way to reach customers, one-to-many content uses digital engagements in product, encouraging users to fully adopt features while building deeper, more meaningful communities. Customers are more likely to renew as their engagement and usage broadens via Community and in-app content. Meanwhile, your internal teams can use their time more efficiently and eliminate continuous outreach tasks.

Digital-led onboarding can accelerate TTV in a scalable way by providing digital user guidance and training (and removing friction) during the onboarding experience. Digital-led onboarding leverages prescriptive journey automation to quickly guide users to value—in product and via Community programs. In addition to improved TTV, Digital-led onboarding can help customer-facing teams save hours of manual outreach and training time. They can also help to maximize account ratios while still ensuring that key milestones are reached in a customer's onboarding journey.

6

Evolving to the Personalized Phase

Personalized Phase

Strategy:	Data-Driven Journeys
Key Use Cases:	Closed-Loop Feedback
	Automated Advocacy Programs
	Prescriptive Adoption Journeys
Tactics:	Persona-Based Nurture Programs
	Automated Advocacy
	Automated NPS Program

In retrospect, evolutionary changes in business and technology can seem preordained. For example, it may seem inevitable today that once humans invented the wheel, they would soon attach axles to the wheels, which they would then attach to carts powered by draft animals, which animals they would later replace with mechanical engines. (On the other hand, as comedian Jim Jefferies noted, nobody thought to put wheels on suitcases until 1971. Said Jefferies: "I remember my father being at the airport carrying two bags with another one under his armpit, like "There's no better way to

93

do *this!*" We went to the airport in a [bleepin'] car. He saw wheels in motion. He was holding a wheel the whole [bleepin'] time. Couldn't piece it together."[1])

On paper, the evolution from horse-powered chariots to EVs powered by lithium-ion batteries looks like a neat and linear progression—one we "naturally" divide into different phases. But in real time, such evolutions are rarely so neat and tidy. To people who live through periods of disruptive technological change—from the invention of the wheel to the development of the internet, B2B cloud computing, and generative AI—"progress" doesn't always appear linear or divisible into discrete epochs. In fact, the changes often appear chaotic, with no guarantees that any particular technology is destined to dominate.

By the same token, your organization's progress through the different phases of Digital Customer Success—from Reactive and Proactive to Personalized and Predictive—may someday appear like a neat, linear progression. But while that journey is underway, you may not even realize when you have transitioned from one phase to the next. Instead, because each stage of digital maturity facilitates the next stage, the borders between phases may be blurred. The tools you adopt and the user data you collect in the Proactive stage will enable you to seamlessly enter the Personalized stage. The tools and data you leverage during the Personalized stage will enable your Predictive phase programs.

To move your organization toward the Personalized end of the Digital Maturity spectrum, you first need to ask yourself: "What is the next thing we want to do with our users?" If you followed our Chapter 5 recommendations regarding Self-Service Enablement, One-to-Many Customer Communications, and/or Digital-Led Onboarding programs, you may already have enough data to adopt the use cases outlined in this chapter. If not, it's time to collect more data around customer personas, usage, and sentiment to enable these programs.

Closed-Loop Feedback Programs

One common complaint among CS organizations is that Product teams, especially at tech companies, tend to examine the market in terms of what to build next—which new feature to build and which new technologies to adopt. In short, Product is biased in favor of new customers over current customers. CS teams, meanwhile, are constantly tugging at the sleeves of Product people and saying, "Hello! We already have all these amazing customers. We need to do right by them. We need to fix something that isn't working. We need to listen to what they want and don't want."

Closed-loop feedback programs offer a solution to this challenge by providing a way to digitally capture more user feedback to inform product roadmaps, improve awareness, and increase adoption at scale. One Gainsight customer, Shiji ReviewPro, experienced a *3,900 percent increase* in its NPS responses rate after switching from email to in-app surveys.[2]

Challenge:

Lack of input from customers and poor feature release communication leads to inaccurate customer health, low adoption, and surprise churn. User feedback and ideas are siloed (or not captured at all), disjointed, and not visible to the Product team to help impact future roadmap decisions.

Solution:

A streamlined and transparent way to collect customer feedback and ideas to make data-backed roadmap decisions, and a way to close the feedback loop and effectively communicate these updates with users/ customers.

Important Personas:

Community Manager
Post-Sales Leader and CS Leader
CS Ops Leader
Education Leader
Product Leader and Product Manager

Before Scenario:

- Customers are unaware of new features that solve pain points/needs, so they do not adopt them.
- Customers have valuable product feedback, but they do not know where to share this information and/or they never hear back from their CSM about their requests.

- Product teams are making roadmap decisions that are not backed by data and customer input.

After Scenario:

- Engaging release communications inform users of new features, leading to higher activation and adoption.
- Customers have specific channels to share their valuable input, submit product ideas, and see their status via digital and CSM outlets.
- Product teams can easily aggregate usage data, survey results, and customer feedback to make roadmap decisions.

Closed-loop feedback programs (aka voice of the customer programs and survey programs) are some of the fastest, lowest-cost ways to ensure that customers are not going off the rails, for aggregating and channeling customer feedback to Product, and for locating customers who are having such a great experience that they are ready to become references and advocates. The process could not be simpler: You ask them one question. *One* question. And from that single question, you build additional processes and automation.

Here's what makes the closed loop so special. As you may know, if you ask customers for input but do not close the loop by following up with a thank-you message (or some other form of acknowledgment) or by responding to the concerns/questions expressed in the feedback, the quantity of feedback that you receive in the future will plummet. Why? Because customers will feel that they are simply tossing their opinions and comments into a black hole. Ideas go in; nothing ever comes out.

But when you show your customers, time after time, that their feedback will prompt you to take timely action—when you demonstrate that you value their feedback by doing something about it—this will cause them to become more engaged. They will soon come to realize that you *always* translate their opinions, challenges, and suggestions into meaningful responses.

We typically launch a closed-loop feedback program with a standard NPS question, such as "How likely are you to recommend our product on a scale of 0 to 10?" (See Figure 6.1.) If the customer response qualifies them

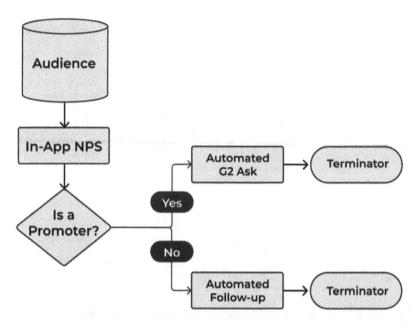

Figure 6.1   Gainsight's flowchart for detractor management.

as a promoter, we then automatically route them to, say, a public review site such as G2.com. (See the "Automated Advocacy Programs" section.)

What about survey respondents who indicate that they have had a poor or mediocre experience? How and when should you respond to them?

We recommend that you develop one or more automated templated responses (see, e.g., Figure 6.2) to acknowledge that these customers are having a poor experience—and we suggest you do this either through your centralized customer hub or through email. Regardless of the channel, draft a note to the detractors that conveys the message: "We've heard you. We collected a lot of your feedback and, in response, here are [two, five, or 10] things we are doing to improve the situation."

In general, you should close the loop in a scalable way that employs both digital- and human-led methods. However, in response to poor scores from your *largest* customers, have your CSM—or even the Chief Customer Officer—send a note manually. Do not send automated messages to your high-spend customers. Save the automated responses for the tail end.

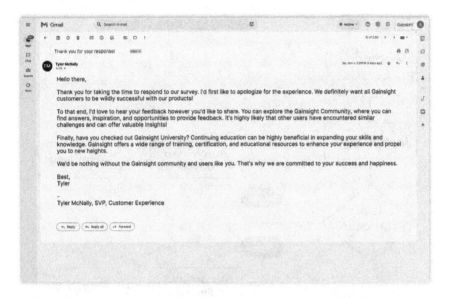

Figure 6.2 Sample email from Gainsight to acknowledge detractor concerns.

One of the greatest benefits of Digital CS is the power to liberate your human CS staff to focus on high-value activities. And intervening with an at-risk, high-spend client obviously qualifies as high value. As much as you might like to, you cannot respond, one to one, to every user or customer, but when it comes to the C-suite of your largest customers, you will probably want to ensure that a human is in the loop. This is what your CS technology can help deliver—a customized blend of human- and digital-led CS motions and activities that fit your organization's priorities and culture.

Closed-loop feedback also offers a significant number of cross-functional benefits. But to enjoy these benefits, you need to think about how you will get the sentiment data to the right teams—product feedback to Product, sales feedback to Sales, and so on. Hence, first you need a way to analyze that data. This is where customer experience solutions can make all the difference. For example, Gainsight offers an AI-powered tool called

Text Analytics, which can sift through all those survey responses to identify and categorize the different themes, helping you review and analyze mountains of survey data in a very scalable way.

In terms of the channels you should use, you can do closed-loop feedback via email or purely in app. (Some of our more sophisticated customers prefer to do both.) At Gainsight, we like to start the process with an in-app survey, and if a customer does not respond within that channel, we switch to an email that says something like "We really want to hear from you, but you didn't respond in app."

What Problem Are You Trying to Solve?

Before initiating a closed-loop feedback survey, be sure to ask: "What problem are we trying to solve for our users by launching this effort?" In other words, develop a problem statement. *Then* ask yourselves, "What are some ways to solve the problem?" Although it can be tempting to rush headlong into a closed-loop feedback initiative without first answering these questions, doing so will increase the likelihood that you will not effectively respond to all that customer feedback. And if you have no plan for what to do with all that feedback, you risk alienating customers by encouraging them to take the time to respond to a survey and then giving them nothing in response—no thank-you messages, no acknowledgment of their efforts, and (critically) no positive improvements to the product in response to their input. Running a closed-loop feedback program like this is worse than not having one at all. Instead of converting customers with poor NPS and CSAT scores into advocates, you could end up undermining your company's credibility.

Not long ago, Gainsight identified two problems based on the results of an admin NPS survey. The admins—the users most responsible for running Gainsight in a customer environment—posted the lowest scores of any type of Gainsight user. In addition, they were not very responsive as a group. So when we in Customer Success asked ourselves, "What problem are we trying to solve vis-à-vis our users with a closed-loop feedback program?" the answer was: (1) we need to increase the number of responses from admins, and (2) based on what we hear, we need to boost their scores (and get credit for doing this). And that is precisely what we did. We said, "We weren't able to get enough responses via email, but we know that admins live in the product. So let's start with an in-app survey and then supplement it with email if we don't receive enough responses."

As a result, our response rate nearly doubled—from 17 percent to 29 percent. With all this additional data in hand, we then set in motion our plan to increase the NPS. We created an admin certification, which— among other things—now provides specific release information just for the admins because they were telling us that they were often unprepared for our releases. (The business people in the customer organization would contact the admin and say, "I want this new feature from Gainsight," and the admin would reply, "I've never heard of that feature.") Our solution was to provide release information to our admins first— before all the other users—in order to make their jobs easier. In addition, we created a destination within our customer hub, tailored specifically to admins, to help them learn from one another, share best practices, and engage in Q&A.

Since rolling out this closed-loop program, admin NPS scores have risen from an average of 31 to 70.

For Gainsight, this was a half-step into the Personalized stage of Digital CS Maturity. In terms of data, all we needed to know was that the survey recipients were admins. That's it. From there, we were able to build a variety of digital experiences tailored to this user group—experiences that resulted in a spectacular rise in positive customer sentiment.

Automated Advocacy Programs

Automated advocacy programs help you identify and engage successful customers in advocacy programs in order to drive new business. Automated advocacy programs help you identify and engage successful customers in advocacy programs in order to drive new business. Businesses typically garner a higher retention rate when customers are referred by advocates. And according to a Harris Poll Online survey conducted on behalf of customer loyalty platform provider Ambassador, 82 percent of consumers say they proactively seek referrals when considering a purchase.

Challenge:

It's a struggle to identify and engage successful customers to serve as references or advocates. Our current programs are highly manual and highly dependent on individual CSM relationships.

Solution:

An automated way to collect user sentiment at scale that allows for immediate identification and engagement with healthy, happy customers, enabling them to engage with their preferred advocacy outlets in Community, reference programs, and more.

Important Personas:
- Community Manager
- Post-Sales Leader and CS Leader
- CS Ops Leader
- Marketing Leader

Before Scenario:
- It's time-consuming to identify and coordinate advocates, which slows down sales.
- Not tracking the degree to which pipeline advocacy programs influence health scores.
- Worried about overusing and fatiguing main advocates with too many requests.

After Scenario:
- Gain a better understanding of our customers' health and relationships as we look to maintain our reference database.
- Scale sentiment collection to identify advocates more quickly.
- Engage advocates more deeply in Community, encouraging them to share their knowledge and input, and remain engaged.

Here's how automated advocacy programs are conducted at Gainsight:

If you are a Gainsight customer who has awarded us an NPS score of 9 or 10, we immediately inject you into an automated flow that says, "Sounds like you're having a great experience. We want others to know about it." We then offer the customer a reward (such as a gift card) to incentivize continued participation in the advocacy process. This process can quickly fill up a review site with raving fans. From there, we have a feed that brings all those G2 reviews into our Slack environment for our executive team to read. Every G2 review is in there.

Why does this kind of advocacy matter? Because by the time most prospects talk with a sales rep, it is *very* likely that they have already looked at that review site and already interacted with some of your customers. Which means that, in many instances, the first impression of your company and its products/services will be made not by your salespeople, not by your product, and not by your marketing content, but by your customer advocates—and you need that first impression to be overwhelmingly positive. You want to stack the deck in your favor.

With this in mind, the accounting solutions firm Floqast uses an automated advocacy process to help identify and incentivize their gold customers. "These are people that we really want to get responses from," says Justin Smith, Global VP of Customer Success at Floqast.

> Let's say our universe consists of a hundred customers. We might first say, "Based on the data we have from our quarterly NPS and other surveys, we're going to contact 70 percent of our customers with automated emails." Once the responses come in, we might then say, "Here's the top echelon of folks that we want to focus on." Now our goal is to drive a lot of responses from these people.

From there, Smith's team might send automated follow-up emails until they've narrowed the list of likely advocates to an elite few. "We'll then target these gold customers with some really personalized incentives to make sure we get them to respond."

Smith stressed the importance of adequately rewarding customer advocates while also avoiding fatigue. In fact, addressing these twin challenges were among the reasons why Floqast launched the automated advocacy program.

People can get fatigued, so you don't want to go back to the well too often. If we have people who are really supportive of Floqast and are being really helpful, we don't want them to burn out. We also want to make sure there's something in it for them. So, we use points and rewards to communicate the message: "Hey, if you're doing this, there's a tangible reward for you." That's been really helpful. It's also created a lot of camaraderie because people, especially self-identified advocates in Community, know what their peers are doing. So we want to make sure that every advocate feels like they're being rewarded in a fair and equal way.[3]

Like Floqast, don't ask just *anyone* to leave a review, particularly a G2 review. Instead, ask *only* those customers who have given your company the very highest survey scores. That way, you'll minimize the chances of a negative or mediocre review.

Prescriptive Adoption Journeys

Question: Once the customer is using our product (after onboarding), how can we get them to adopt the features that are most likely to help them achieve their goals?

Answer: Prescriptive adoption journeys. This use case creates an end-to-end user experience that personalizes communications, with the goal of guiding customers to value faster.

Challenge:

Customers receive disjointed communications that do not effectively guide them to value in our product, resulting in low adoption, higher churn, and negative sentiment.

Solution:

A single, unified experience for customers across digital and human touchpoints via programmatic digital engagements. This improves adoption and enhances the overall experience by providing the right message in the right channel at the right time, facilitated by accurate data.

Important Personas:

- Community Manager
- Post-Sales Leader and CS Leader
- CS Ops Leader
- Education Leader
- Product Leader and Product Manager

Before Scenario:

- Customers receive generic (or no) support in navigating products to find value, resulting in low adoption.
- Customers are constantly relying on their CSM to provide recommended usage or actions.
- CSMs are highly reactive, answering repeated questions or spending extensive time with each individual customer.
- No clear, prescriptive "learning path" has been designed to help guide the customer along their journey.

After Scenario:

- Customers receive communications specific to their needs that help them reach value faster.
- CSMs spend less time on repetitive tasks and instead engage in high-value activities.
- Customers have a better overall experience, receiving key guidance when and where they need it.

At this stage of the customer's journey, there are two things you really want to avoid: (1) low adoption and (2) adoption for adoption's sake. In the second case, you risk promoting usage that appears healthy, with the buyer saying: "Everything is great! All my people are logging in to your product." Getting users to log in to your product is not the goal. Your goal is to understand how many users are extracting value from the product and how many are not, thereby revealing whether the customer is at risk of churning. If you push adoption of features that you consider "core," but those features are not aligned with the customer's goals, you are guiding the customer down a dead-end street. By contrast, prescriptive adoption journeys are goal-focused. You set aside your own views regarding how the product should be used, and, instead, you map out an adoption journey based on each customer's desired outcomes and experiences.

In most respects, prescriptive adoption journeys are similar to the adoption journeys you are already using, with one key difference: You are personalizing them. And to achieve the level of personalization that we recommend, you will need more data.

If you don't know how people are using your product, you can't map out a prescriptive adoption journey. You need *usage* data. You need to know how people are using the product, so you can either encourage them to adopt it or, if their usage has fallen off, bring them back into the fold. Contrast this with one-to-many communications, where you don't need any data to get started. With prescriptive adoption journeys, you need at least two or three pieces of data—you need to know how the customer is using the product, which goals they are hoping to achieve, and every user's role (in order to send the right information to the right people).

If you don't know who the users are, start by asking about their role, and then guide them to adopt themes that align with their goals. If you don't know their goals, you could conduct an in-app survey that asks: "What is your main focus when using our product?" If the user responds by saying "Goal X," you can then route them to "Feature X."

At Gainsight, we send a weekly adoption email to every customer. Instead of having a CSM meet with the customer to share this data whenever they ask, we *proactively* send them this data via email. This allows their business leader and CS Ops person to determine whether they are on track or falling off the rails vis-à-vis adoption.

How Drift Guides Customers to Value

What can SaaS companies do to really drive customer value realization? At Drift, a conversational cloud company that helps businesses automate their sales processes, the answer is: use customer data to improve how we engage with those customers.

As Scott Ernest and Bart Hammond of Drift explain:

> It's about more than a high-touch, human-to-human experience, but about making the experience personalized and contextual. How do we drive that intimate moment of interaction that will propel adoption? How do we make it easier for customers to do business with us? How do we empower them through information? How do we nurture them through education? How do we cultivate advocacy that will drive us forward?

Before teaming with Gainsight, Drift's team of 70 CSMs focused on delivering an "incredibly high-touch" (but one-size-fits-all) experience to each of its 5,000 customers. After purchasing Gainsight's CS product, the company aggregated all the information around Drift into a unified 360-degree view of the customer. From there, CS built an automated health score that proved to be highly indicative of renewal and expansion, and Drift started using that health score to collect even more information from customers, including NPS feedback around onboarding and support experiences.

Ernest and Hammond continue:

> We then rolled out a paid Customer Success model with different entitlements and SLAs for different customers because we needed to treat each one of them differently. We also started using Timeline as this amazing activity-tracking and SLA-commitment engine. Then our CS Ops teams built these amazing dashboards that literally became the cockpit from which our CS people do their jobs.
>
> "With all this information and health data and insight, we began to find patterns in adoption and health that we wanted to tackle. Like many companies, we are very focused on our "golden features"—those unique advanced features that are compellingly different and truly differentiate us from other chat platforms. So we began to run campaigns to ensure that our customers are leveraging those advanced features. We started with Journey Orchestrator, doing the typical email response forwarding to our customers to drive them to take the next action, but then we created a Digital CS function. We procured the Gainsight product analytics and engagement product, and we've been doing in-product feature announcements, leveraging tool tips, and even letting users sign up for events at which they can learn more about Drift.

The thing that excites Ernest and Hammond most is the recent revamp and relaunch of their Community via the Gainsight Customer Hub platform.

> Prior to that, it was shocking how stale and outdated that Community had become. But after launching the new Community, the customer response was overwhelming. I've seen customers come out of the woodwork to talk about the insights they've gotten. It's really cool to see how this hub is really energizing people—and you can't imagine the energy that's coming out of badging and gamification. We have people fighting to see who can be the Drift Knowledge Thought Leader.

More recently, the company rolled out an evergreen campaign, which it calls the Sales User Win-Back. Explain Ernest and Hammond:

> It all started with Journey Orchestrator, which allows us to see which of our customers hasn't logged in in the last 21 days. We wanted to drive them to a one-to-many webinar that would educate them, getting them to take some great next action, whether that was updating their notification settings to get alerts on their mobile devices, or enrolling them in an outreach sequence, or recording a video, or connecting with them on LinkedIn. It was great! We got lots of adoption.
> We also learned that email alone is insufficient. So once we drove them to the website, the next thing we did was partner with our product organization to improve the landing page and really customize the experience of logging in, delivering a real "wow" moment for users. Then, rather than forcing people to go back to the email to register for an event, we now have a pop-up in-app that lets them register for that event right there.
> What we found is that we were able to take the recording of webinars and other events and post them to the Community—in tandem with a little digital goodie bag of best practices and examples of how you can get more value from Drift—and provide that as an experience to the attendee, as well as to registrants who didn't make the event, and even to new users who just signed up for Drift and are looking to get more value.
> Overall, we have created a kind of virtuous circle—this iterative growth circle—which leverages a variety of human and digital programs.[4]

Strangers in a Strange Land

Always remember that at the beginning of the adoption journey, your customer is a disoriented stranger wandering through a strange new land. When they first adopt your products, they are overwhelmed with new terms and features and may not know where to start. Therefore, it's up to you to meet them where they are on this journey and guide them in an efficient way so they don't get lost and give up. You can provide a digital map for your customers, no matter how complex your products are. You can easily get them to their destination, with the right guidance.

Digital Customer Success allows you to understand the desired user journey and deliver an effortless experience to your customers as you help them reach their final destination of unlocking continuous value.

Let's take a look at how this can work, using the hypothetical example of a SaaS company that serves the healthcare industry: Energy HR. At this company, Anthony Plant is responsible for scaled Customer Success, and thanks to his Digital CS solution, he has an overview of every customer that's currently in the adoption stage. But now he wants to improve the digital journey for his customers.

With the right AI-powered tool, Anthony can quickly determine which new features will lead to healthy and strong user adoption. In fact, the AI quickly identifies three different program options that should help Anthony to set up and deliver in-app guidance to users so they can easily launch the feature. Anthony chooses a program from among the options and instantly sees the audience criteria that the AI suggests, as well as every step that might be valuable for users to take—via in-app engagement—as part of this prescriptive path.

From here, Anthony can preview this engagement directly from this program and also set goals that he intends to deliver for the actual program engagement. In this case, he wants 50 percent of all the users to click through that engagement within the first three weeks. Once he sets that goal, he can simply hit "save" before publishing the program. But before he does that, he heads back to the AI to give it one more command: "Let's provide users who set up and launch this new feature with a badge. Let's give them a moment of joy to celebrate the accomplishment." Once Anthony sees the badge that he has in mind, he reviews and then publishes the program.

One of the chief benefits of this CS solution is that it takes some of the work off the admin's shoulders while still giving them control over the process. That's because this technology is not designed to replace humans but to ensure that they can more efficiently support their customers' needs.

Ten years ago, the scenario we just described was still the stuff of science fiction. Today, it is a reality that you can deploy and enjoy right here and right now.

Summary

Lack of input from customers and poor feature release communication can lead to inaccurate customer health, low adoption, surprise churn, and missed opportunities for customer growth due to a lack of value. Too often, user feedback and ideas are siloed (or not captured at all), disjointed, and not visible to the Product team to help impact future roadmap decisions.

Closed-loop feedback programs offer a solution to this challenge by providing a way to digitally capture more user feedback to inform product roadmaps, improve awareness, and increase adoption at scale. A streamlined and transparent way to collect customer feedback and ideas, these programs are a way to close the feedback loop and effectively communicate the updates with users/customers.

Automated advocacy programs help you identify and engage successful customers in advocacy programs in order to drive new business. If your current advocacy program is highly manual and highly dependent on individual CSM relationships, it can be a struggle to identify and engage successful customers to serve as references or advocates. An Automated Advocacy Program collects user sentiment at scale, allowing for immediate identification of, and engagement with, healthy and happy customers. The program also enables customers to engage with their preferred advocacy outlets in Community, reference programs, and more. In addition to helping you scale sentiment collection to identify advocates more quickly, automated advocacy programs enable you to gain a better understanding of your customers' health and relationships.

Once a customer is using your product, how can you get them to adopt the features that are most likely to help them achieve their goals? Prescriptive adoption journeys. The use case described in the text creates an end-to-end user experience that personalizes communications, with the goal of guiding customers to value faster. At too many organizations, customers receive disjointed communications that don't effectively guide them to value in the product, resulting in low adoption, higher churn, and negative sentiment.

Prescriptive adoption journeys provide a single, unified experience for customers via programmatic digital engagements. This improves adoption and enhances the overall experience by providing the right message in the right channel at the right time. Facilitated by accurate data, customers receive communications specific to their needs that help them reach value faster; CSMs spend less time on repetitive tasks and instead engage in high-value activities; and customers have a better overall experience.

7

Evolving to the Predictive Phase

Predictive Phase

Strategy:	Intelligent Experiences
Key Use Cases:	AI-Driven Risk Management
	Programmatic Value Realization
	Optimized Expansion Selling
Tactics:	Capture verified outcomes
	LTR survey
	Preventive risk alerts

By the time you reach the Predictive phase on the Digital Maturity Spectrum, you are ready to design (or are already designing) intelligent customer experiences powered by omnichannel technologies that propel customers to successful outcomes at lightning speed. By combining digital channels with great processes and data, your organization can finally take advantage of AI and data science to identify at-risk customers *far* in advance, increasing the likelihood that your clients will renew and expand. With these tools, you can identify and predict customer behaviors with astonishing accuracy and then tap your teams' digital-fueled superpowers to continually optimize the customer journey—and your own.

AI-Driven Risk Management

If you've been in this business for any length of time, you know that the "straight and narrow" path to successful outcomes is lined with potentially catastrophic detours—lots of them. You also know that some detours are more common, and more dangerous, than others. Again and again, you see customers slipping and falling off the path at the very same place.

What can you do to prevent slips and falls before they happen? And when they *do* happen, how can you put things right?

This is where AI-Driven Risk Management comes to the rescue. This use case helps you automate at-risk customer programs based on usage and sentiment, enabling you to proactively flag and engage customers to overcome risks.

Challenge:

Customer risk scoring is not accurate. It is based on only a few signals and is missing key, granular data around adoption, sentiment, and product needs. Risks are not proactively addressed and/or the current programs are manual and time intensive.

Solution:

A scalable, more granular way to capture data-driven churn risk, automate at-risk customer programs, and align teams around key product roadmap needs.

Important Personas:
- Post-Sales Leader and CS Leader
- Product Leader and Product Manager
- Community Manager
- CSM

Before Scenario:
- Organizations do not have visibility into key risk factors, resulting in surprise churn.

- At-risk customers are not effectively engaged to reduce and overcome risk in a programmatic way.
- Customers' product needs are not well captured or communicated, resulting in new churn risks.

After Scenario:
- Organizations gain a full picture of customer risk by incorporating usage, health, sentiment, and product-request data in one place.
- At-risk customers are automatically engaged via digital and human touchpoints to address risk factors and realize value.
- Product teams effectively prioritize roadmap items to reduce major customer churn risk factors.

If you're a successful Gainsight customer, you may have appointed one or more people to a systems owner role to optimize the use of our products. From our vantage point, this is a sign of good customer health. We've discovered that customers who appoint a systems owner are less likely to churn. Therefore, once we became aware of this data point, we created a signal that alerts us to the absence of a Gainsight systems owner within a customer's organization.

The moment we learn that a customer has not appointed a systems owner, or that the person has resigned, been terminated, or otherwise left the company, we know the customer is at risk of churning. (And, using predefined signals, it doesn't take long for us to detect the absence of the systems owner. If we don't see this person appear for a specific length of time, we receive an alert that basically says: "We think this person is gone. Send an email to the business stakeholder to confirm whether this is true." If the business stakeholder replies to the email by saying, "Yes, she's gone," we send the stakeholder another note that says: "We have options for you in the short term," including (but not limited to) paying for a systems owner on demand. At a minimum, we'll say: "Who on your team could start learning Gainsight? Let's get them on the certification path."

This entire process is completely automated—start to finish. As soon as we receive the signal that the admin is gone, a series of communications is triggered in an effort to persuade the customer to appoint a new systems owner ASAP.

You can set up a similar process for admins and any other stakeholders you wish to track.

How would you respond today if a business sponsor left the customer's organization? In this instance, the first challenge for many CSMs is that they may not learn about the sponsor change for quite some time. In fact, the CSM may be the last to find out that their key contact quit, mentally checked out, or was fired. To address this issue in the future, you could adopt a CS platform that automatically keeps tabs on key personas. For example, the Gainsight version of this product (Sponsor Change Alerts) searches LinkedIn updates to keep tabs on your sponsor. (See Figure 7.1.) If your sponsor is named Tom, and he leaves your customer's firm, Waystar RoyCo, to join GoJo, you immediately receive an alert that says: "Tom has left Waystar RoyCo and is now at GoJo."

Prior to AI-Driven Risk Management, Gainsight CSMs were responsible for most of the work described earlier. When we saw that an admin had left a particular customer, one of our people had to engage in a series of email communications, forward admin certification information, and so on. Today, this all happens without any CSM involvement—yet another instance of high-value strategic work that no longer requires any human effort.

The trick to this use case is to first determine which customer behaviors are key risk factors and then to create the right signals to alert you

Figure 7.1   Gainsight's AI-powered Sponsor-Tracking feature.

when a customer is engaging in those behaviors. Otherwise, a certain amount of surprise churn will be inevitable because you won't have visibility into key risk factors and, therefore, you won't be sure what the corresponding risk signals should be. Thus, you need to establish the right signals up front. Then, once the signals are in place, you could ask your CSMs to respond manually every time they receive an alert, but an automated process for managing at-risk customers will save them countless hours on their computers and phones, freeing them to pursue other high-value activities.

Once again, you will want to treat your largest customers differently. In these cases, it's best not to put them through the automated process. Instead, allow your automation to identify and notify you about potential problems, after which your CSMs can spring into action.

Programmatic Value Realization

This use case addresses the question of how to sell *value*, rather than feature functionality, during the sales process, as well as how to deliver on your value promises. Programmatic Value Realization aims to improve retention and growth by ensuring that your customers achieve value from your organization, guiding them more prescriptively to their desired outcomes. According to Bain & Company, a seemingly modest 5 percent increase in retention can account for a 95 percent increase in profits.[1]

Challenge:

Lack of visibility into desired customer outcomes makes it challenging to guide users to value. Customers have no insights into key metrics or ROI, which makes it challenging to understand the value of the product and prevent a churn risk.

Solution:

Capturing and validating customer needs to deliver tailored digital and human communications. This prescriptively guides users to value, at scale, and continually surfaces ROI for improved visibility. Achieving verified outcomes is about driving customers to their next set of goals, opening the doors for new use cases/needs, and results in expansion and growth.

Important Personas:
- Community Manager
- Post-Sales Leader and CS Leader
- CS Ops Leader
- Product Leader and Product Manager

Before Scenario:
- Organizations do not have insight into specific user goals or the changes to these goals over time.
- Customers do not receive guidance that is prescriptive to their needs. As a result, they do not adopt the features needed to realize ROI.
- Customers are not readily aware of the outcomes they are realizing, resulting in a perceived lack of value.

After Scenario:
- Capturing user goals gives vendors and customers visibility into objectives and progress toward ROI.
- Customers can more quickly reach value through automated journeys, key knowledge base content, and Community.
- Customers can easily surface the ROI achieved to internal stakeholders to prove out product value.

In theory, Programmatic Value Realization is simple, but, in practice, many companies struggle with this use case. The main stumbling block is determining how to evaluate success during pre-sales so that the moment someone becomes a customer, you can map out a journey that is sufficiently aligned with—and provides sufficient visibility into—the customer's progress toward their goals and objectives.

One way to achieve alignment and visibility is to employ a digital survey tool that enables prospects to identify their goals, after which the AI will provide recommendations on how to achieve them. Once the salesperson confirms these goals and recommendations, this data is automatically migrated into the CS platform. Now both the sales and post-sales teams know exactly why this customer bought your product. By knowing that, you can set up automated systems and processes tied to those goals.

Case in point: A few years ago, a new customer might come to Gainsight with 10 goals, five goals, or no goals whatsoever. Unfortunately, there was no consistency to what the sales reps recorded or how much detail they provided to the post-sales teams. Obviously, this type of system is not scalable, so our next step was to create a digital data-capture system—in the form of a survey—to help us improve our proactive value selling.

Thanks to this data-capture system, hand-offs from our sales to our post-sales people are smoother and more seamless than ever. No longer does a CSM start a kickoff meeting with a new customer by asking "So . . . why did you buy Gainsight?" and then turn beet red upon learning that the customer has been repeatedly discussing their goals with salespeople and account managers over the past six months.

The best practice is to start capturing and tracking customer goals during the actual sales process via your CRM platform. The second-best practice is to survey the customer during the sales process. And for low-spend customers, these processes can be completely automated using in-app surveys.

As soon as the opportunity is closed, send a survey. Then, based on the information revealed by the survey, your post-sales people can show up to their first meeting with the customer looking smart, well informed, and well prepared. So if a customer tells us that their goal is adoption, we will say, "Great! There's an adoption webinar coming up at which you can learn about how the fleet management platform Dealerware (see Chapter 4) saw its adoption improve by 100 percent using Gainsight. And there is also an in-app guide to driving adoption with Gainsight." (See Figure 7.2 for an example of how Gainsight's in-app survey appears to users.)

Optimized Expansion Selling

Optimized expansion selling gives you a way to automate identification and engagement with cross-sell and upsell expansion plays—at scale—and avoid missed opportunities. Thirty-eight percent of organizations leverage usage data to identify expansion opportunities, according to Gainsight's PLG Index 2022, and 20 percent of revenue for top SaaS organizations comes via expansion, according to a SaaS Unit Economics Report.[2]

Challenge:

Our CS teams miss or do not engage programmatically with upsell or cross-sell opportunities. A lack of proper triggers/understanding

Figure 7.2   Gainsight in-app survey.

results in missed revenue to the business and the perception that CS is a cost center for the organization. When opportunities are captured, our teams are highly reactive, often delayed in engaging, and do not have the prescriptive workflows needed to be successful.

Solution:

A way to scale expansion through multichannel programs that drive cross-sell and upsell revenue. These programs proactively identify customers via data and organic Community engagement and trigger automation to facilitate expansion.

Important Personas:
- Post-Sales Leader and CS Leader
- CS Ops Leader
- Account Executive and Account Managers
- CSM
- Community Manager

Before Scenario:

- CS teams do not have a way to automate expansion plays. As a result, they are reactive, missing key opportunities.
- Expansion programs are spread across the organization, leading to siloed information and duplicated efforts.
- Expansion programs are high touch and time consuming, and lack personalization.

After Scenario:

- Teams can proactively identify expansion opportunities and kick-start cross-sell and upsell programs.
- Cohesive and multichannel programs can be executed using CSQLs and PQLs to capture, land, and track the expansion revenue generated from CS initiatives to surface value.
- Scalable digital expansion programs are easily automated and eliminate missed opportunities, ensuring that revenue isn't being left on the table.

Imagine that your newest customer has done everything needed to be successful right out of the gate. They have completed your digital onboarding program, and, since then, you have been supporting them with adoption programs to ensure they receive maximum value from what they use. Is there an opportunity to sell more? Maybe this customer purchased three modules, and all three modules display healthy usage. But your company offers two additional modules that the client has not yet purchased. This may be the perfect time to reach out to them and say, "Did you know that if you add this other module, you can expect to receive X value? You are already making great use of the three modules that you bought." In other words, if you know the customer is already employing a, b, and c use cases, they are probably ready for the next set of maturity workflows. By nurturing these workflows, you can open up a discussion on the purchase of additional products, licenses, modules, and the like.

This is just one technique you can use to drive expansion opportunities from the usage data you have collected. Another key strategy is to use a freemium/paywall model, like those employed by companies such as Zapier, Gong, and Calendly, where the model is built into their products. These companies are very smart about saying, "Look at all this data you could access if you upgraded your subscription!" For PLG companies like these, this is business as usual, but for software companies like Salesforce, this is terra incognita.

Digital solutions can give SaaS companies the ability to create paywalls and freemium experiences without having to use their own engineering resources. They provide non-product-led growth organizations with all the capabilities of a PLG company. Are you tracking usage? Are you doing in-app engagements? Are you guiding people to value? If the answers to those questions are *yes*, are you then upselling them—perhaps with in-app teasers that say, "This feature is paid. If you want to see more, let us know"?

Dealerware does something very much like this. Whenever they identify a promoter based on their NPS score, they dive deeper into that customer's usage and say, "This client just awarded us a 10. They love Dealerware and they are *really* using the product." The company's next step is to serve the customer an upsell campaign directly in app. The client receives a pop-up that says, "Check out this new module that will provide A, B, C value."

And it works!

It works very well. In fact, in their first experience with this campaign, a single in-app message generated $128,000 in upsell revenue—far more than they paid for the CS product that enabled the campaign.

Dealerware also leveraged their Digital CS to obtain 100 percent visibility and adoption as well as an astounding 2,700 percent increase in NPS response rates. Previously, they were getting very poor response rates from their emails, but those in-app messages turned everything around.[3]

In terms of the data needed to effectively execute the three use cases in this chapter, you need to add risk-management signals, you need to know the user's role, you need to know usage, and you want to know sentiment. If you know who the prospect/customer is, what they are doing, and how they feel, this will give you confidence to put them into either a risk program or an expansion program.

The Role of AI—Today and Tomorrow

As you evolve into the Predictive stage, AI will assume a more prominent, and more sophisticated, role in your Digital CS programs.

But what exactly *is* that role, and how will it evolve? Answering such questions can be a tricky, caveat-packed endeavor, and—like a freshly peeled avocado—the use-by date of our forecasts will probably arrive sooner than expected. Still, we think it's important to share our thoughts, with the caveat that nobody really knows where we'll be a year from now.

That said, here is one forecast that we are confident in making: *AI, especially the newer generative AI technologies, will make customer self-service much more powerful.*

Imagine that you have a library of amazing content to help your customers, but the content is scattered and disorganized. Your customers must diligently search the entire collection to find what they need. So right now, this resource falls into the category of "nice to have, but a huge pain in the neck."

To make life easier for your clients, you introduce a card catalog. Okay, that's a laudable improvement, if still time-consuming. Then you decide to introduce a federated search capability that can scan the entire library in a matter of milliseconds to locate exactly what your customer needs. Better, right?

Now imagine that instead of a search capability, you give the customer an "instant-answer machine"—an AI-powered tool that, after reading the contents of your library, gives your customers the answers they were seeking in the form of a coherent narrative. By doing this, you will increase the value of your content library by many multiples.

And this capability already exists!

If your content library is composed of hundreds of Community posts and thought-leadership articles, and you aggregate the data into a corpus that the AI can access and from which it can continuously learn, you will have an instant-answer machine that is as intelligent and knowledgeable about your products and services as any human—only much faster and much better at multitasking.

Some Gainsight customers are already introducing these instant-answer machines. In the summer of 2023, for example, the experience management company Qualtrics was preparing to unveil an AI-powered Chatbot that provides article summarizations for customers. "It will appear like a human-led conversation supporting the entire product," said Kari Ardalan, Global Head of Digital and Scale Success. "From there, we're working toward using the capability for ticket interception and live agent handover." The questions then become: "Which tickets would still need to be forwarded to a human? Could we use AI to mimic human interactivity, bringing in a human only when we need one?'"

Although Ardalan and her team are making rapid progress, many other questions must be answered before AI can assume a bigger role within Qualtrics CS and Support.

Where we were once focused heavily on UI and UX of the support portal, we now wonder, "Should we simply use an AI smart search to search everything? Is UI and UX as important anymore? How do we use ChatBots for our CS frontline engagement? And how do we bring AI, not only into our product, but into our self-service use cases too?

We're also looking to AI for a ton of internal use cases. Writing our content, our guides, because our content team is always strapped. At the same time, we don't want to lose the creativity that humans bring to the table, so that's a risk. You don't want to over-digitize things, because if everyone's getting an AI-powered email or interactions, is that authentic anymore? Maintaining a balance between human creativity and machine capabilities will be a challenge.

In addition, Ardalan and her team recognize that there are security risks that must be addressed before AI-fueled tools can be safely rolled out. For example:

You don't want to pump so much data in there [the AI] that a competitor could simply ask, "How do I beat Qualtrics on a deal?" and gain a competitive advantage. Obviously, we need to lock that down. We need to decide which data will, and will not, be pumped in there.[4]

Ardalan is right to be concerned about the potential security risks posed by AI, as well as the perceived authenticity and actual quality of machine-generated content. Not long ago, our president for products, technology, and global operations, Karl Rumelhart, learned just how easily AI-generated responses can become FUBAR (F—ed Up Beyond All Recognition) rather than fantastically futuristic. Karl met some members of another company's Customer Support team at an international conference—a team that had used AI to improve customer self-service. They initially thought, "We should be good because we have 4,000 knowledge-based articles in our database. We'll have the AI read the content and then answer questions."

It was a disaster. As it turned out, most of those 4,000 articles were out of date, contained inaccurate information, or had some other type of flaw. As a consequence, the Support team had to put everyone to work for several weeks to weed out all the "bad" content. Eventually, they condensed the library to just 800 articles, and once that was done, the AI performed perfectly. Today, their self-service is working even better than the team originally anticipated.

The caveat here is that *the quality of the responses generated by AI depends on the quality of your data.* Garbage in, garbage out.

This caveat also applies to the problem of *AI hallucinations.* You ask the AI a question, and it responds with an answer based not on its training data but from out of the blue. Here's an example recently uncovered by the *New York Times*:

> The lawsuit began like so many others: A man named Roberto Mata sued the airline Avianca, saying he was injured when a metal serving cart struck his knee during a flight to Kennedy International Airport in New York.
>
> When Avianca asked a Manhattan federal judge to toss out the case, Mr. Mata's lawyers vehemently objected, submitting a 10-page brief that cited more than half a dozen relevant court decisions. There was Martinez v. Delta Air Lines, Zicherman v. Korean Air Lines and, of course, Varghese v. China Southern Airlines, with its learned discussion of federal law and "the tolling effect of the automatic stay on a statute of limitations."
>
> There was just one hitch: No one—not the airline's lawyers, not even the judge himself—could find the decisions or the quotations cited and summarized in the brief.
>
> That was because ChatGPT had invented everything. . . .
>
> [The] program appears to have discerned the labyrinthine framework of a written legal argument, but . . . populated it with names and facts from a bouillabaisse of existing [unrelated] cases.[5]

How do you avoid this problem?

By asking the AI to answer questions on the basis of *clear data.* If you ask the system, "How old is Nick?" without clarifying which "Nick" you mean—that is, without giving the machine any specificity or context—the AI will not know who you mean but will still try to answer the question. It would be great if the machine could respond to the query "How old is

Nick?" by replying, "Can you be more specific?" but that day is not yet here. For the moment, it is up to the user to phrase the question in a way that will minimize the likelihood of a hallucinatory response.

Why are we focusing on this issue? Because accurately *and automatically* tracking people is something that tech engineers have been working on for a long time. For the most part, they have become pretty good at tracking usage. But in the future, AI will need to accurately track specific *individuals*, and that is a much more difficult task. Why? Because it is harder for AI to differentiate between the "Nick" who serves as CEO of Gainsight and any of the other million-plus "Nicks" living in the databases to which the AI is connected.

In general, tracking individuals is a thornier problem for B2B firms like yours than for B2C companies like Amazon because an individual customer might spend decades with the same Amazon-associated identity. By contrast, the way we normally view a person in a B2B environment is in the context of their *company*, because that's what our customer is. Therefore, when someone moves from the customer's company to a different firm, the AI identifies them as a new and different person. (As you saw earlier in this chapter, one way that Digital CS tries to work around this challenge is by associating individuals with organizations that make them appear more "stable" in the mind of the AI—organizations such as LinkedIn.)

Another forecast we are confident in making is that *AI will enable organizations to have a massive impact on Customer Success, leveraging the work of relatively few employees.* The caveat to this prediction is that those few employees will need to be very sophisticated when it comes to working with AI—for some of the same reasons just mentioned. Among other things, they will need to consistently provide AI-powered systems with clear, high-quality data to ensure that your company is targeting and tracking the right people and then *automatically* delivering the right messages, at the right times, to those people. If one of your employees makes a tiny error when it comes to a single one of those elements—right people, right message, right time—it might throw a big monkey wrench into your onboarding, expansion, or advocacy campaign.

You have probably encountered this sort of mistake in your personal life. One evening, you decide that you are done with those scuffed brown shoes in the closet. So you do a search on your mobile device to locate a spiffy new pair. After a little browsing at one or two sites, you locate a new pair that matches your tastes perfectly, and you buy them.

Then you decide to scan the headlines on that same mobile device. Almost instantly, advertisements appear in every article for the very same shoes that you just bought. This is an excellent (and very common) example of the right person, right message, *wrong time*. You already took the action that the AI is now prompting you to take.

Fortunately, it will soon be easier to operate AI technologies.

For example: If your intention *today* is to send a survey email, and then—if the customer does not respond within five days—to deliver that same survey in-app, and if the customer still does not respond, to deliver the survey via another channel, you must manually instruct the system (from the get-go) to follow that series of steps.

But in the not-so-distant future, your system will have the ability to automatically follow that same procedure, as long as you tell the AI: "This is my intention." The system will understand exactly what you want to do with a minimum of input. In a sense, the system will predict all the steps you wish to follow based solely on your desires.

What role will AI play in the future when it comes to predicting the behavior and intentions of your customers?

Well, this brings us to the third, and final, forecast that we can make with a high level of confidence: *AI will empower organizations to automatically generate and deliver the most relevant content to the right individuals at precisely the moment they need it.*

The way we think about the situation today is this: One of the simplest ways of communicating with customers is to build a website and then direct your clients to that site via email. "Hi, everybody, look at the great content that we just uploaded to the website!" If, however, you want to get a bit more sophisticated, you could stagger the emails so that different users receive them at different times. "Hi, admin, the release notes on Feature X are now available, for admins only, on our website." This approach is a little more sophisticated in the sense that you are communicating with users at the times when that information is most relevant to them. You are differentiating with regard to the time when different users will receive the *same* information.

But then you might think, "I shouldn't send the same release notes to every user. Maybe I should send different packages of information to different segments of my customer base, with small businesses receiving Package A, medium-size businesses receiving Package B, and so forth.

From there, the next step might be to differentiate based on individuals—the thousands or tens of thousands of individual users who work at your customers' companies.

Imagine generating tens of thousands of unique emails, texts, or in-app messages—each one tailored, in terms of both content and delivery time—to every one of your users. This is what AI will be able to do with a minimum of human input. Instead, based on the data already in the system, the CS platform will know that Janice is in X stage of her user onboarding journey and respond accordingly with multichannel communications.

Or, maybe the customer is a longtime client but has just started using the product and is not used to a particular feature. The AI-powered platform will "know" not to discuss topics with which she is not yet familiar. (That might cause her to feel insulted.) Instead it will wait until she reaches the next stage in her onboarding journey before sending her the next round of training information.

Achieving this kind of predictive prowess may require additional technological breakthroughs, and it *will* require that you collect a lot of data. Who is Nick, really? Who is Kellie, really? What are the differences between them? What are they doing? With such data, you can be much more predictive than you are today. You will know "What would be the best thing to write in this next message? What is the best offer to make next? What is the best advice to give, and the best action to suggest?" A variety of technologies promise to accomplish this, including predictive analytics and generative AI. We have not yet reached this level of sophistication, but this is the path we are on. This is the promise we are working to fulfill.

Summary

The path to successful outcomes is lined with potentially catastrophic detours—some of which are more common, and more dangerous, than others. Often you see customers slipping and falling off the path at the very same place. What can you do to prevent slips and falls before they happen? And when they *do* happen, how can you put things right?

Too often, customer risk scoring is not accurate because it's based on only a few signals and is missing key, granular data around adoption, sentiment, and product needs. Risks are not proactively addressed and/or the current programs are manual and time intensive.

AI-Driven Risk Management provides a scalable, more granular way to capture data-driven churn risk, automate at-risk customer programs, and align teams around key product roadmap needs. With this use case:

- Organizations gain a full picture of customer risk by incorporating usage, health, sentiment, and product-request data in one place.
- At-risk customers are automatically engaged via digital and human touchpoints to address risk factors and realize value.
- Product teams effectively prioritize roadmap items to reduce major churn risk factors.

Lack of visibility into desired customer outcomes makes it challenging to guide users to value. Customers have no insights into key metrics or ROI, which makes it challenging to understand the value of the product and prevent a churn risk. Programmatic Value Realization captures and validates customer needs to deliver tailored digital and human communications. This prescriptively guides users to value at scale and allows them to easily surface the ROI achieved to internal stakeholders to prove out product value.

Sometimes CS teams fail to engage programmatically with upsell or cross-sell opportunities, resulting in missed revenue to the business and the perception that CS is a cost center. When opportunities are captured, teams may be reactive, delay their engagement, or lack the prescriptive workflows needed to be successful.

Optimized expansion selling provides a way to scale expansion through multichannel programs that drive cross-sell and upsell revenue. These programs proactively identify customers via data and organic Community engagement and trigger automation to facilitate expansion. With these programs, teams can proactively identify expansion opportunities and kick-start cross-sell and upsell programs.

As you evolve into the Predictive stage, AI will assume a more prominent, and more sophisticated, role in your Digital CS programs. Exactly what that role will be is difficult to predict, but we can confidently say that AI will:

- Make customer self-service much more powerful.
- Enable organizations to have a massive impact on Customer Success, leveraging the work of relatively few employees.
- Empower organizations to automatically generate and deliver the most relevant content to the right individuals at precisely the moment they need it.

8 | Launching Your First Digital Initiative

You can change your attitude, you can change your approach to a problem, you can strategize.

—Canadian astronaut Chris Hadfield

Checklist

- When designing your first Digital CS initiative, pick a manageable starting point rather than trying to solve every problem at once. Choose a single moment in the customer life cycle and build from there.
- Develop a clear program charter by answering questions such as "What's our objective? What problem are we trying to solve?"
- Choose a single main metric that will enable you to determine if you're making progress.
- As you move forward, keep an eye on your velocity and beware of scope creep.
- Determine which customers or customer segments to start with, as well as which user personas.

- Adopt a three-phase approach to testing and learning.
- Choose digital channels that are best suited to driving the behaviors you want to see from your target customers and personas.
- Keep an eye on your bandwidth by judiciously deploying your people and other resources.
- Think about how to scale digital journeys, programs, and communications—and how to scale your CS teams.
- Meet your customers where they are.
- Evaluate success and iterate tactics in the early stages of the Digital CS program.

Launching a spacecraft into orbit, and keeping it there, requires an alignment of three factors: thrust, velocity, and altitude. Thrust is the amount of force needed to propel a spaceship off the launch pad; velocity includes not just speed but also course corrections; and altitude is about how close to the planet the spacecraft should fly.

Likewise, launching a successful Digital CS motion requires alignment of the same three factors: thrust, velocity, and altitude. Although we believe Digital CS is the future of our industry, it isn't a space race. Quite the contrary. Successful digital programs often move at a slow but steady pace—gradually building toward a single, specific, attainable goal.

Choose a Single Life Cycle Moment

As you begin planning for liftoff, we strongly suggest that you pick a manageable starting point rather than trying to immediately solve every problem. In other words, start small. Instead of trying to engineer a grand digital program that encompasses the entire customer life cycle, choose a single moment in that life cycle and build from there.

Years ago, we worked with a customer who tried to tackle everything at once. They were so keen to incorporate Digital CS that they created, in advance, an email for every moment in the customer life cycle—a period of three years! We had to (gently) explain that this was an exercise in futility.

Given how rapidly software solutions evolve, by the time that customer reaches the six-month point in the life cycle, all those prewritten emails will be hopelessly out of date. For this reason (among others), it's best to focus on one moment in the life cycle, not an epoch.

The first (and often overlooked) customer experience with your product after the sale closes is the "welcome email." In many ways, this is *the* moment of truth. Because this is their first experience as your customer, it sets the tone for the rest of the relationship. If the welcome email is confusing or lacks meaningful substance, you're setting your customers down a risky path. Our early versions of welcome emails were text-heavy, packed with platitudes about "joining the family," and had very little practical value. Today, our welcome emails are designed to jump-start the user and customer journey. (See Figure 8.1.) They quickly communicate specific setup steps that would normally have to wait for the first meeting and also focus on creating self-serve habits:

- How a user gets started today with a Gainsight product
- A basic high-value use case the user can start working on
- An invitation to learn more from us and other customers in our community

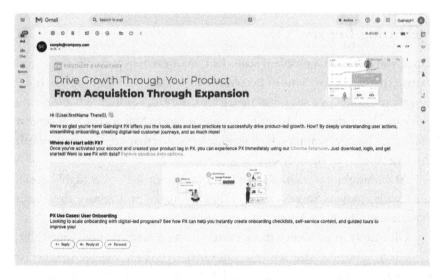

Figure 8.1   Gainsight welcome email.

In Digital CS, generating enough thrust to achieve "escape velocity" from your current condition requires a well-constructed launch pad—in the form of a clear program charter. So as a first step, ask yourself, "Why are we getting started on this path? What's our objective? And what tactics will we use to achieve that specific objective?" (*Note:* In addition to articulating the desired impact on the customer's business, analyze that impact from the perspective of your teammates and investors.) This will help you form a clear program charter and articulate your goal in a way that the entire company will understand.

You may recall that we once identified a problem with our customers' admin users. (See Chapter 6.) We learned that many of these people were struggling with the more mature use cases of our tool. They were unaware of all the resources that we had created to help them and also lacked clear guidance on how to access those resources. In response, our first step toward creating a Digital CS program charter was to articulate a "problem statement"—a simple and *narrowly defined* synopsis of the issue. We did *not* cover every user type and customer persona in the statement because we had not identified a problem with every user type and customer persona—only with the admins. We decided to tackle one problem at a time, and so should you.

Measuring Impact

Once you settle on a problem statement, the next step is to choose a main metric that will allow you to determine if you are making progress. It can be easy to drown in a sea of 30 metrics, so, instead, consider what outcome you care about the most. Identify the single North Star metric you want to focus on. Then determine which leading indicator maps to that outcome. In this case, there can be only one.

At Gainsight, for example, we realized Admin NPS was highly correlated with renewal. So we crafted a digital journey to improve the Admin experience, which we know has a real impact on our bottom line.

Ultimately, your ability to succeed will be determined by your ability to collect, interpret, and leverage customer data, in a scalable manner, to measure the impact your program is having on customer behaviors. As you wrack your collective brains to select the best metric for measuring your first program, here are a few things to keep in mind.

Choose a Leading (Not a Lagging) Indicator

Although the ultimate goal of every CS program is achieving positive NRR, that metric is a lagging indicator. In general, lagging indicators tell you: "Congrats! You've done something right," or "Oops. You did something wrong." What they rarely tell you is what the "something right" or "something wrong" actually was. And without this knowledge, you can't make data-driven refinements or course corrections to your program. To determine what's working and what's not, you'll need to select metrics that serve as leading indicators—metrics such as:

- **Reach:** Did we manage to identify and reach the right users?
- **Effect:** Did we manage to persuade these users to engage in the desired behaviors?

The right leading indicators will help you predict and influence lagging indicators, such as ROI. For example: The VP of Marketing [Reach] adopted Feature X [Effect] and decided to add three more seats to their plan [ROI].

Pick a Milestone That Matters Most to You

To identify the best leading indicator, look to your customer journey milestones. Once you know what these milestones are, you can determine which data points you're able to track against those milestones and select one that matters most to you. For example, during the onboarding phase, the most important data points will likely be:

- How quickly you are onboarding customers
- How well you are onboarding customers
- How quickly customers see value from your solutions

And within these larger data points, there are smaller, more specific questions that you can ask—questions that can help you uncover more granular data. These include:

- Are we reaching the right users?
- Are we using the right channels?
- Are we reaching out at the right time?

- How effective is our current content? (Do customers take the actions we want?)

Then, during the adoption phase, you will want to know:

- Are customers successful in using the product? (Are they achieving desired outcomes?)
- Are customers using our key product features? (And do they understand the value of those features?)
- Are customers using *all* of the features they paid for?

Keep It Simple

To avoid being buried in superfluous data, be clear about what you're looking for and what you want to achieve. Again, keep things simple. Focus on the data points of just one goal that you want customers to achieve during their journey. And remember: Your main metric should be one that gets you closer to your goals. Once you determine how to deliver the right content to the right users at the right time, you will start reaping the rewards.

Beware of Scope Creep

As you move forward, be vigilant for any signs of scope creep. Whether it takes the form of putting too much on your plate or becoming so exuberant about an early win that you rush to build another initiative, scope creep is a killer of digital initiatives. "Wow! We did such a great job with the new welcome email! Think of all the other things we could do. Let's crank out more emails." Before you know it, you are trying to address (via email) every problem experienced by every user type and persona at every stage of the customer life cycle.

In addition, keep an eye on your velocity. Ask yourself, "How fast is reasonable for you to go?" Moving too fast may hinder your ability to make course corrections as you build. Moving too slowly may counteract your thrust, leaving your pilot program stuck on the launch pad.

Note: If you don't already have a clear point of view of what your non-digital life cycle looks like, we advise you not to build a digital program just yet. You should have a point of view about the experiences that a healthy customer has on the way to achieving their outcomes and renewing. *Then* you can think about how digital tools can change the delivery of those outcomes.

Which Customers and Personas?

As you consider which moment in the life cycle to focus on, you also want to determine which customers or customer segments to start with, as well as which user personas. This may be harder to do than it sounds. If you're accustomed to having human CSMs cover every customer, the idea of "surrendering" control may create anxiety—for both you and the customer.

In our experience, the key is to start with situations, customers, and personas that represent a low risk, build your confidence, and then expand the program. This means, for most SaaS companies, starting with the lowest-spending segment of clients. To manage the risks even more, you might want to conduct a pilot program that includes only new clients so you can establish the proper expectations for the digital program on Day 1. As for personas, you might want to start with the more technical personas, such as system admins—people who tend to be open to a digital experience.

Over time, you will then expand the program's scope to include more customers and personas. As you do, you may discover what so many of our customers already have—that higher-value personas (such as executives) are much easier to reach digitally or are *only* reachable digitally. Contrary to their pre-digital expectations, many SaaS companies also learn that their largest clients want some parts of the customer journey to be self-service. Ultimately, expanding your digital programs across the entire base helps you extend your reach for all customers, whereas CSMs are primarily engaging with only a handful of key stakeholders.

Before rolling out a digital program, we recommend that you adopt a three-phase approach to testing and learning:

- **Phase 1:** Experiment and test with the smaller-spend digital customers. This is where you can run AB tests to learn what's working and what's not.
- **Phase 2:** Once you obtain successful test results—and you believe the digital program or engagement will be net neutral or net positive for the rest of the customer base—the next phase is to roll out the program to all your customers. From here, additional refinements can be made, as needed.

- **Phase 3:** It's now time to fully operationalize the program, transforming it from an isolated initiative into an ongoing program that is embedded in the customer life cycle.

Use Different Channels

Now that you've chosen the issue you wish to address, the precise moment in the life cycle at which you will address it, and the customers and personas you want to reach, it's time to start thinking about the digital channels you will use to drive the behaviors you want to see from those customers and personas. As you start developing the channels for your Digital CS program, here are a couple of things to consider:

- Which channels are you currently using, and which ones work well for you?
- Which channels are likely to be the most effective in driving the behaviors that will help you reach your goal?

To help facilitate a decision, you may want to consult your product roadmap and carry out an audit. Look at key customer behaviors and ask the following questions:

- What actions did customers take to achieve the key behaviors?
- What channels did they use? Is there a pattern?
- What type of content did they really engage with? Did that content cover certain sections of our product or areas of interest? What can we learn from that?

If you have enough data to identify trends, use that data as a baseline to develop your channels and the content you're pushing through them. Otherwise, work with the data you have, and iterate as you learn more about your customers and their preferences.

Bear in mind that every touchpoint is an experience, and your goal is to make each of those experiences a positive one. Therefore, another way to get started vis-à-vis choosing channels is to simply ask the customer. Ask what works for them. Do they want email prompts? In-app guides? Or would they be happier to self-serve using a knowledge base? There's never a wrong time to ask customers about their communications preferences, so do it consistently to understand how their preferences might change as they mature with your product.

Alternatively, depending on the size of your organization, your available resources, and your digital maturity level, the channels decision may have to be based (at first) not on customer preferences but on which ones would be the easiest or most cost-effective to implement *right now*. Although a centralized, multichannel digital customer hub (see Chapter 5) is an excellent self-service enablement tool, it's not a must-have. If you lack the resources (financial or human) to manage such a platform, or if you need a quick-and-dirty way to immediately address customers' common questions and pain points, you could start with a no-frills Community platform that features nothing more than help articles and Q&A. Driving customers to this resource, in this format, is better than offering them no self-serve options at all.

And at this point, don't worry too much about production values and other cosmetics. Think about the value that your users will derive from your digital resources rather than the packages those resources come in.

Whichever channels you end up choosing, please avoid the mistake of thinking: "Well, we have this email capability, so . . . let's use email!" The next thing you know, every single digital motion you create is an email. And the next thing your customer thinks is "Wow! I got five emails from my vendor this week. I'm not going to look at any of them. In fact, I'm going to start archiving them." Before long, your emails are ending up in spam folders worldwide.

Choose Channels Best Suited for the Target Audience

Put serious thought into what the right channel is *for each audience*. Consider why or how someone would use a channel before deciding that every touch should be an email or in app.

For example, when you want to conduct NPS surveys with end users, your default channel should probably be in app (whereas email is usually a better default channel for executive stakeholders). For end users, the product is where all the magic happens. It's the central component of their customer journey and experience. So when you're engaging with end users, search for ways to keep everything in the product. Think of how you could turn the product into a one-stop shop not only for solving pain points but also for answering users' questions.

Historically, many people equate Digital CS with one-to-many email campaigns. And email *is* a good tool. However, given the amount of "noise" that occurs in email today, this channel is more likely to be ignored by end users than in-app messages. In addition, the product is what customers are paying for, and it's where users spend a great deal of time. Thus, in-product communication can help you meet users where they live and where they are in their journey. Are they in the onboarding stage, the adoption stage, or in year two of renewal? Are they light users, advanced users, or superusers? What is their persona? All these factors should contribute to your decision regarding which channel(s) to choose and when to communicate.

In app is an excellent way to help customers realize value very quickly. Whereas email may contain more content than some recipients are willing to read, and Community requires an effort to log in, engage with other members, and ask questions, in-product communication doesn't require users to lift a finger. They don't have to log in to a website or pick up the phone. They can stay put, which is an ideal customer experience for many of them. And if the behavior you're trying to drive centers on *using* the product, then in-app communication is the way to go (whereas Community makes more sense when you're aiming to drive peer-to-peer networking).

Using in-product messaging, you can provide a checklist to your users based on where they are, guiding them to the most valuable actions they should be taking. You can also use in-product experiences to develop awareness of new features rather than emailing release notes. You can then drive them to adoption of those new features and use in-app surveys to capture feedback on how relevant or useful the release was and whether they adopted it or not. In short, the whole release experience could take place within the application itself.

You can even use your product to facilitate event registrations or drive customers to additional channels. (And you can do this without risking "notification fatigue" by automatically limiting how many in-app messages certain users receive during a particular time period.)

Sometimes it might make sense to deliver a blended digital-channel experience. For example: You might start the onboarding journey with emails (to get people into the product in the first place) before transitioning to in-app checklists and walkthroughs. From there, you could encourage users to engage with your Community or customer hub for additional training and peer-to-peer networking. Some users will be happy—even eager—to interact with their peers via a Community platform. As we said in Chapter 2, do *not* underestimate the value of Community. When it comes to giving customers the ability to self-serve within a single, personalized, automated journey, there's no better tool than Community-based peer-to-peer connections.

Initially, these interactions might be limited to basic Q&A. But over time, they can evolve to the point where your Community platform evolves into a multichannel customer hub—a centralized destination encompassing Community, Customer Education, Knowledge Centers, and more, which is curated to create a personal experience for the user. Among other things, the customer hub enables users to engage in virtual (and sometimes in-person) meetups and roundtables and for individual thought leaders to create and distribute articles and videos. (Today the Gainsight Community even includes an off-platform Community that our admins launched for themselves on Slack. Thus, we no longer think of Community in terms of just the platform itself but in terms of the relationships we are fostering between different customers and between different customers and ourselves.)

Creating a successful Community doesn't happen overnight, but when you get it right, it won't just take the load off your CSMs but will also serve as a central hub for your customers to access everything they need to reach more value milestones and, in return, yield the business outcomes they were promised.

Although a mix of channels often achieves the best results, be careful. The channels you use should work together to help the customer unlock value, not make them lose sight of what they're trying to achieve because of message overload.

Keep an Eye on Your Bandwidth

As you plan your first initiative, keep an eye on your bandwidth. Assuming you have a limited number of CSMs on your team, and not an army, choosing where to deploy your people and other resources is a question you must answer up front. The last thing Digital CS should do is create a bandwidth problem. Digital CS is here to *extend* the bandwidth of your team. But it can be easy to lose control of the scope of your program if you say *yes* to every idea that comes your way. To protect yourself and your team, get used to saying "Not right now" or "We're not ready for this" or "Do we need to deprioritize something else?"

Thinking about how you can frame those trade-offs to your business partners is critical. They might observe your situation from the outside and say, "Come on! It's just a simple mail campaign," whereas *you know* just how much effort that simple email campaign requires in order to effectively prompt users into taking the right actions. Even the simplest email campaign involves a lot more than drafting a few paragraphs of copy.

We've said this before, but it's worth repeating: Do *not* try to do everything at once. Do not try to tackle all the altitudes—all the orbits—simultaneously.

Focus on one particular customer or user segment, preferably an essential segment. Determine the unique needs/problems of that segment, and then choose the digital experiences that will most benefit them. In addition, select use cases that will produce the most yield for both your business and the customer's business—for example, increasing adoption of your product's golden features. Think of your customers as sitting along the Digital Maturity Spectrum. As a vendor, you can turn the dial up or down on the level of digital experience they receive. Over time, you can then turn control of the dial over to them so that individual users select the blend of digital- and human-led experiences that they want.

Strive for Runaway Accretion

Returning to our space-themed analogy, here's a bit of jargon that may prove useful: *runaway accretion*. Runaway accretion is the process by which a large mass in space draws matter to itself, causing it to grow bigger and draw in even more matter. This continues until the object becomes so massive that its powerful gravity can pull in matter from great distances.

To put this in Customer Success terms: If your digital initiatives are doing well, your high-touch CSMs should be thinking, "Why is digital not in my segment? Why are my customers and users not getting this experience? They need it!"

Runaway accretion is another way of saying *momentum*. As one trial succeeds and is embedded into the customer life cycle, you then go bigger, testing more pilots, embedding more of them into the life cycle, and so on. You can then go back to your leadership and say, "We tested a new process, and this is the result we're seeing. From there, we're adding yet another digital experience.

Go big, and bigger, and then bigger . . .

One of the many great things about working at Gainsight is that everyone is encouraged to experiment. As a result, we have conducted experiments with many different teams, including those focused on driving journeys in Product Experience. We have consolidated some of these learnings in the remainder of this chapter, with an eye on the Digital CS tactics that have proved most successful.

Based on our experiences, we believe the best way to jump-start a digital program is to start with the data you have, however limited or imperfect. From there, look for opportunities to refine your existing data and to acquire additional (and more specific) information. As Okta's Melissa Allen told us:

> There's always going to be something that *could* hold you back. But you have to start somewhere. And once you start, you'll be amazed at your instant learnings. And from there, you can pivot, you can iterate, and you can build.
>
> A couple of years ago, we didn't have half the data points we have now, and we wouldn't have learned which data points we needed until we started to find out what was working and what wasn't. That's the thing. You've got to take that first step. You learn and then realize "Ah ha! *Now* I know where to go next, thanks to all these learnings." So, start somewhere. If you don't try, where are you going to end up?

For Allen, choosing a life cycle moment to address with the first digital program was a no-brainer.

> It was definitely onboarding. If you don't get them early—either new admins in an old system, or new admins in a new system—then they're not going to be sticky. They're not going to understand what they bought. They're not going to understand all the features that are at their fingertips. So if you do only one digital thing, catch these folks in onboarding and make them feel like they know what they're doing. Make them feel comfortable with the product—with all the cool stuff they now have at their fingertips.[1]

At the start of Gainsight's digital journey (the Proactive phase), we employed generic one-to-many emails and in-app communications. These communications included a monthly newsletter from Nick, as well as a monthly CCO newsletter, and did not require specific account, user, or persona data to execute. These programs helped us grow our database and facilitate higher engagement. They also helped us test the effectiveness of different content in terms of what was resonating and what was not.

Our next step, which brought us into the Personalized phase, was soliciting our customers' help in collecting more data—information that would assist us in personalizing their experience. "Here's the list of contacts we have for your organization. Can you confirm if these people are still with your organization, and still in the same roles?" Sixty-four percent of our customers responded to these requests for help.

In addition, CS worked with our Product team to change the login process for one of our products. We made it a two-step login process. Thereafter, every time a user signed up for the first time in the product, we displayed a brief, two-step survey that helped us gather more data. (And the response rate for this survey was 95 percent!)

These tactics helped us build rich data around the customers and users in each of the account bases. And that helped us personalize a lot of the content and programs moving forward, helping us drive adoption. Emails received by the right people increased by 5 percentage points. The open rate rose by nearly 6 points, and the click rate climbed 7.5 points.

It took a few quarters to build the data, but through these tactics, we were on our way to runaway accretion and toward the threshold of the Predictive phase.

Ready to Scale?

Once you build out your first digital program, the question becomes "How do I take this to the next level? How do I scale?"

Keeping in mind that Digital CS is a spectrum that combines the digital with the human, we recommend that you think about scaling in two ways:

- How can I scale my digital journeys, programs, or communications?
- How can I scale my CS teams? What are the key milestones along the user journey at which I can provide a blend of human and digital touchpoints at scale?

At Gainsight, one of our first scaled initiatives was a simple welcome email that was part of our onboarding program. Every new user received an email that essentially said, "Welcome. We are very excited to have you aboard. Here are five steps to get you started." Over time, we made refinements to the onboarding program and the email. Today, we have a welcome email that is beautifully designed, specific to each customer, and personalized by user role. But we didn't build this overnight. It evolved over time.

Today, we also have a multichannel strategy that includes our customer hub, where all users can consult an in-app knowledge bot and new users can refer to an onboarding checklist. (See Figure 8.2.) We also employ a pooled CSM model, as well as highly specialized and very personalized emails, as part of the onboarding program.

How about scaling your CS teams? We get a lot of customer questions about how we structure our own Digital CS teams, especially "What does your org structure look like?"

We've seen three common types of org design emerge for Digital CS programs. (See Figure 8.3.) Getting started typically begins with a cross-functional steering committee approach. Because subject matter experts (content, in app, one-to-many campaigns, Community) are often spread across the org, the group usually comes together as a virtual organization. Over time, this group tends to evolve into a centralized and dedicated team—typically reporting to the CCO. Finally, capabilities are embedded into multiple functions.

Figure 8.4 shows an example of a Digital CS org chart.

At Gainsight, we have three different teams, each specializing in specific areas, and our CS org structure is built around those teams.

Team 1 is in charge of life cycle programs. They are focused on understanding key milestones in the customer's life cycle and experimenting with different campaigns to see what resonates—which content is working, which channel is having the most impact, and so on. Their work provides us with a framework to validate results that drive success at scale.

Team 2 is charged with the experience program. Their main job is to think about the end user's journey and experience, bringing multiple channels into the fold and considering what the end-to-end journey and experience should look like. This team organizes events to support content creation, advocacy, and engagement.

For example, we have identified features that make our customers very sticky. After examining the data, we concluded that if a customer uses five

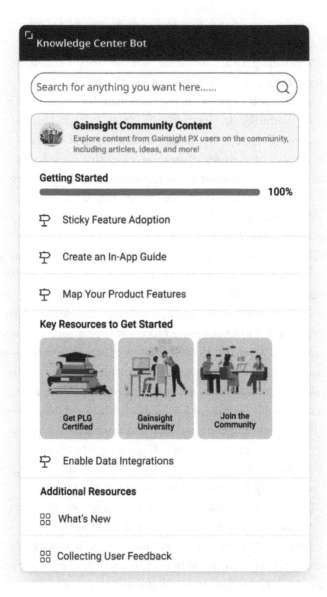

Figure 8.2 Example of a Gainsight onboarding checklist.

specific features, retention is definitely higher. These features make customers super sticky and less likely to churn. Our next step, therefore, was to look at the adoption data around these five features across accounts. After doing this, we chose three features with account adoption under 50 percent, and

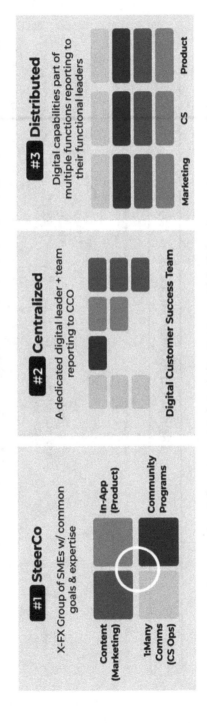

Figure 8.3 Three common types of org design for Digital CS programs.

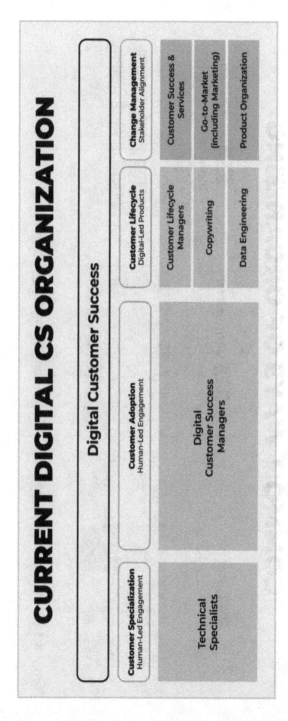

Figure 8.4   Example of a Digital CS org chart.

from there, we worked with our CSMs to develop programs to drive higher adoption.

Ultimately, we determined that a combination of office hours, in-app guides, and email campaigns, each focusing on one particular feature over the course of one month, was the key to increasing adoption of all three features. And we didn't stop there. We continued to track the adoption of each feature over the next quarter to make sure that every uptick was a sustained increase, not a temporary blip resulting from one of our recent pushes.

Finally, Team 3 is composed of our pooled CSMs, who focus on delivering outcomes for customers at scale through proactive outreach—such as with best practice recommendations. They also serve as active listening posts as we unveil new digital experiences and programs.

Collectively, these three teams, all possessing similar subject matter expertise and overlapping goals, drive our customers' Digital CS journeys and programs by developing proposals on the most impactful activities and scaled programs that reduce churn and secure renewals, maximizing the time available to our CSMs for high-value activities.

Popmenu Offers Four Steps to Start Improving Your Efficiency via Automation

For CS organizations struggling to accomplish more with less, learning how to automate and scale low-impact processes is key to unlocking greater efficiency. In her presentation at Gainsight's 2023 Pulse Conference, Jess Kitt, former Vice President of Client Experience at Popmenu—a leader in cloud-based restaurant technology—offered four steps to help you identify early automation opportunities in your customer journey.

Launching a first digital program can be a daunting task, prompting many CS leaders to think, "We're not there yet. I don't even know how to get started."

So how *do* you get started?

Here are Kitt's recommendations:

Step 1. The first thing to do is review your customer journey. We know we need to look at our customer journey for each of our segments. We need to document the core activities aligned to each phase, and review these for each segment, putting this down on a whiteboard . . . and saying, "Here's what we are working with."

Step 2. Look at these activities and identify an opportunity to automate—to bring more efficiency to your team and "protect your magical moments." I like to think of magical moments as the high-impact practices in which you're building a bond with your customers, and you don't want to take those away. You still need those. You still need the human element in your Customer Success work, but you could automate everything around those magical moments, maybe before or after them. [While doing this,] it's important to identify the activities that you don't want to automate as well as those you do.

Step 3. Once you have everything documented and you have developed ideas of what could be automated, you're ready to face the biggest challenge faced by most vendors. Regardless of their best-laid plans, CS leaders tend to believe they don't have enough data, or enough clean data, to put those plans into effect. So once you identify what you want to do, you need to ask, "How are we going to do this? What are the data sources that we need?" Do not get discouraged if you are not yet able to accomplish certain goals. Instead, determine what you can do—what is possible right now (especially the low-hanging fruit)—and start with that goal.

It may be something very small, but if it's a step in the right direction, start building out a plan. Build up those Lego blocks to create a Digital CS strategy that is empowered with automation.

Step 4. Continuously improve. I see customers who get so focused on step one, two, and three, that they completely forget about step 4. And when I say continuously improve, I mean make sure that when you build out the strategies in these automations, determine how well they are working. Are they doing the thing we want them to do? Put a process in place to evaluate them to ensure they're effective—that they're making a positive impact on bringing efficiency to your team.

Which automation opportunities are best suited to basic, proactive motions? In other words, what are some examples of low-hanging fruit that companies should consider harvesting first?

Usually these opportunities are found near the start of the customer journey, with the first being onboarding. Said Kitt:

> We see this a lot. Our CSMs are sending an email welcoming or introducing themselves to a customer, and we think, "We can't automate that because we want it to be personal and we want it to be humanized. We want customers to feel warm and fuzzy when they get that email." But there's still an opportunity to automate."

That opportunity can be found in CS solutions that allow CSMs to automate a more personalized communication.

For example, a good Digital CS platform will enable CSMs to insert unique facts about themselves into their welcome emails, giving customers a personalized feeling when they read that email.

> CSMs spend time with the customer understanding what they are trying to achieve and the value they are trying to get out of your product or service. If your CSMs are getting on the phone to do this, think how you could automate this process to create more efficiency. [Leveraging your CS solution,] you might send a pre-survey to your customers: Tell them about the outcomes you want them to achieve, have them give you feedback, and then automate their responses into a success plan . . . that the CSM owns and drives forward.

Another stage of the customer journey that is often packed with automation opportunities is the adoption phase. Historically,

> CSMs initiate an email thread to coordinate an EBR. They go back and forth and back and forth with the customer: "When are you available? When am I available?" Our team struggles with this. It's an inefficiency—this back-and-forth, trying to find a good common time. What we could do, though, is automate the process. Automatically send an email so many days before we want to have an EBR. In the CS platform, we could add the CSM's calendar and booking link . . . and then tokenize that link into the email so that we put it on the customer to book a time that's convenient for both parties, with the goal of meeting within such and such a timeframe. Maybe you give them a few weeks to do that.

Here's another good opportunity. A CSM receives a CTA play-book when a support ticket is escalated. (Many vendors are trying to build a 360-degree view of the customer, bringing in data from lots of different sources, support data being one of them.) An opportunity that many vendors pursue is to automate a CTA and playbook when-ever a ticket, or a certain number of tickets, has escalated within a certain time frame. We're currently collaborating with a company . . . that is using AI to analyze tickets to let us know, in advance, when the ticket is going to escalate. We're trying to leverage this technology to bring more efficiencies to our teams.

Again, don't forget about step 4. It's so important for us, espe-cially our CS Ops teams, to look at the automations we're putting in place and ensure that they're doing what we want them to do. This is a continuous improvement model that we call "Plan, Do, Study, Act," and it follows the framework outlined above. We first want to plan: We want to identify what we could automate. Then we build out an automation program within our CS solution. After it's deployed, we study it to ensure it's working. Is it doing the thing we want it to do? Is it making an impact on our CS organization to be more efficient? What are the findings? How could we tweak it or improve it? Finally, we will take those improvements and apply them to the development of a new plan that will make the program even better.[2]

Meet Your Customers Where They Are

"Omnichannel communications" and "omnichannel programs" are ubiqui-tous terms in our industry, but they are really nothing more than fancy ways of saying, "Meet your customers where they are." If they prefer emails, give them emails. If they live in the application, give them in-app communica-tions and guidance. Another way of saying this is that you need to deliver strategies, at scale, via multiple channels, that reach the right audiences with the right content at the right times.

If you find yourself devoting a lot of effort to ensuring that your com-munications are uniform in style, tone, and format and you begin thinking, "This isn't the best use of our time," think again. Think from the recipient's perspective. If you were a customer who was receiving content that didn't even appear to be from the same company—content that was unfocused in terms of the actions it was trying to prompt and the priorities it was emphasizing—you would probably get very confused, very quickly. (Keep in mind that the expectations of B2B customers are rapidly catching up to those they have as B2C customers.)

The quality of your messaging matters. Design matters. We have seen how much it matters time and again, which is why we are so diligent today about producing consistently high-quality editorial and graphics content across our omnichannel programs.

At the end of the day, though, launching your first digital initiative is about getting started, and getting started is about developing a point of view regarding your current situation. What's the key business challenge or opportunity? What do you want to change about it? How are you going to change it? Find your starting points. We got started with a welcome email that, in retrospect, seems rather primitive. It consisted of just a few lines of text, with no graphics. But sending out that first email was better than not sending one at all and allowing a customer to think: "What the? I just spent $50,000 on this product and, 24 hours later, I haven't heard a peep from anyone at Gainsight." You never want to put the customer in that frame of mind.

Finally, don't forget to evaluate success and iterate tactics in the early stages of launching your Digital CS program. Making small corrections as you go allows you to scale faster in the long run. In addition, be sure to frequently check your altitude. Ask yourself, "What level are we operating on with this Digital CS initiative?" Don't try to take on all of the following at once:

- Life cycle stage
- Segment
- Product level
- Channel

Get started at a lower altitude and ascend from there, eventually taking on more journey stages and segments as you scale. With practice, you'll figure out where to turn the dial up or down on digital.

When you start small and set your team up for success, the possibilities to grow that sphere of influence become attainable, and the opportunities to drive value are incredible. By leveraging advanced analytics and AI-driven insights, organizations can reach new heights of customer satisfaction, retention, and advocacy.

Summary

As you begin planning your first Digital CS initiative, we recommend that you pick a manageable starting point rather than trying to immediately solve every problem. Start small. Instead of trying to engineer a grand digital program that encompasses the entire customer life cycle, choose a single moment in that life cycle and build from there.

The first (and often overlooked) customer experience with your product after the sale closes is the welcome email. In many ways, this is *the* moment of truth. Because this is their first experience as your customer, it sets the tone for the rest of the relationship. A good welcome email is designed to jump-start the user and customer journey.

In Digital CS, generating enough thrust to achieve escape velocity from your current condition requires a well-constructed launch pad—in the form of a clear program charter. As a first step, ask yourself, "Why are we getting started on this path? What's our objective? And what tactics will we use to achieve that specific objective?" This will help you form a clear program charter and articulate your goal in a way that the entire company will understand.

Once you settle on a problem statement, choose a main metric that will allow you to determine if you are making progress. Consider what outcome you care about the most. Identify the single North Star metric you want to focus on. Then determine which leading indicator maps to that outcome.

To determine what's working and what's not, you'll need to select metrics that serve as leading indicators—metrics such as:

- **Reach:** Did we manage to identify and reach the right users?
- **Effect:** Did we manage to persuade these users to engage in the desired behaviors?

The right leading indicators will help you predict and influence lagging indicators, such as ROI. Once you know what these milestones are, you can determine which data points you're able to track against those milestones and select the one that matters most to you. Your main metric should be one that gets you closer to your goals.

As you move forward, be vigilant for signs of scope creep, and keep an eye on your velocity. Ask yourself, "How fast is reasonable for you to go?"

Moving too fast may hinder your ability to make course corrections as you build. Moving too slowly may counteract your thrust, leaving your pilot program stuck on the launch pad.

Next, determine which customers or customer segments to start with, as well as which user personas. In our experience, the key is to start with situations, customers, and personas that represent a low risk, build your confidence, and then expand the program.

Before rolling out a digital program, we recommend that you adopt a three-phase approach to testing and learning:

- **Phase 1:** Experiment and test with the smaller-spend digital customers. This is where you can run AB tests to learn what's working and what's not.
- **Phase 2:** Once you obtain successful test results—and you believe the digital program or engagement will be net neutral or net positive for the rest of the customer base—the next phase is to roll out the program to the entire customer base.
- **Phase 3:** Now it's time to fully operationalize the program, making it an embedded part of the customer life cycle moving forward.

From here, it's time to start thinking about the digital channels you will use to drive the behaviors you want to see from those customers and personas. Put serious thought into what the right channel is *for each audience.* Consider why or how someone would use a channel before deciding that every touch should be in app or an email.

Keeping in mind that Digital CS is a spectrum that combines the digital with the human, we recommend that you think about scaling in two ways:

1. How can I scale my digital journeys, programs, or communications?
2. How can I scale my CS teams? What are the key milestones along the user journey at which I can provide a blend of human and digital touchpoints at scale?

Meet your customers where they are. If they prefer emails, give them emails. If they live in the application, give them in-app communications and guidance. Deliver strategies, at scale, via multiple channels, that reach the right audiences with the right content at the right times.

9

Company-Wide Digital Program Governance and Cross-Functional Collaboration

---

Checklist

- Establish a Digital CS programs team with a dedicated leader. This team will function as a central committee that sets company-wide CS goals, develops strategies, and recruits and oversees subsidiary tiger teams.
- Assign each tiger team a particular digital initiative, and, if need be, break the team into smaller execution teams to oversee deployment.
- To staff the Digital CS programs team and tiger teams, look for people who can represent the different arms of your business.

- To keep your teams focused on specific, tangible, and achievable objectives:
  - Align them around a limited number of projects.
  - Develop a shared, cross-functional framework as well as a shared scorecard.
  - Create project milestones with cross-functional reviews and sign-offs.

- For certain initiatives, determine who owns tracking and instrumentation, in-product experiences and messaging, and strategy and approvals.
- Solicit executive buy-in by demonstrating the value that the teams will deliver.
- Share the work of your cross-functional collaborations with, and report the results of their initiative(s) to, everyone across the company.
- Obtain a Digital CS platform that enables at least one of these channels: email automation, in-app communications, and Community and/or customer hub.

We've long preached that Customer Success needs to be a company-wide initiative rather than a siloed function. Although few people on the receiving end of our sermons disagreed with this view, most never became converts either. Instead, silos continued to rule the day. And as more CS organizations began incorporating digital technologies, use cases, and channels, existing problems persisted—and were sometimes magnified. That's because the only thing worse than a siloed CS organization is a siloed CS organization with digital superpowers. With their newfound ability to do more with less, CS teams were better positioned to "compete" with communications from Product, Marketing, and Support. The result? More spam in customer inboxes and more customer confusion wrought by dueling messages and scattered resources.

To this day, outdated sales models continue to drive a wedge between the functional teams at many SaaS firms. Old habits die hard. For years, businesses worked within a sales-driven SaaS model, spraying messages across the market in the hope of landing one-off sales. The processes of the growth-at-any-cost era are still impacting SaaS companies, even those that have adopted sustainable-growth models. For instance, your Sales team will be working within its CRM software to close deals. Your Marketing team may have its own set of data to qualify leads and the like. The problem here is that siloed roles often filter into the customer experience, causing a disjointed Customer Experience (CX). And a disjointed CX = a bad CX.

This was the environment that Kari Ardalan encountered at Qualtrics (see Chapter 7) when she took the helm as Global Head of Digital and Scale success in October 2022.

Said Ardalan:

We had all of these resources in different groups. My hub team and Community team sat in Support; the digital team sat in [Customer] Success. The scale front line was in [Customer] Success, but it had a different leadership group. Everything was very, very siloed. We also had a ton of sites—XMI as our thought leadership site and Basecamp as our training site—but nothing was uniting all of them. Our customers were saying "You just keep sending me to all these websites with no clear journey."

So when Qualtrics brought me on board, the goal was "Let's bring all these teams together and start getting some synergies from them all. Why is Community running on its own if we also have a self-serve portal? There should be multiple entry points from these different websites to the materials that we have." We also wanted to establish a single owner for our post-sales communications because we had people sending out multiple newsletters. It was completely disjointed, and no one was thinking about the entire journey moving together.[1]

In the book *Customer Success*, Nick used an analogy to describe the relationship between vendors and customers in the pre-CS era. The relationship, he said, was like that between two boats drifting side by side in a lake, with no one in either boat. Inevitably, the two boats will not remain side by side. Someone has to be in at least one of the boats (preferably both), using the oars to keep them close together. It is the job of CS to operate the oars in at least one boat.

Now imagine that instead of one or two CSMs operating oars, a dozen people from departments across the company jump into the boat, each with their own equipment—oars, kayak paddles, and outboard motors—and begin steering the boat in different directions. *This* is what the relationship between vendors and customers looks like in the absence of cross-functional collaboration. Each function sets its own goals, uses its own metrics, and communicates its own messages to the same customers. At best, the result is a disconnected customer experience. At worst, the result is chaos.

To prevent this, every team throughout the organization must start pulling in the same direction, at the same time, with the same equipment.[2]

Cross-Functional Collaboration Gathers Steam

SaaS leaders began to recognize the need for greater cross-functional collaboration in the years just before the pandemic, and the trend accelerated after the tech downturn arrived. As new sales slowed and tech leaders realized that the only way to maintain revenues was to retain existing customers, many companies switched focus from net new sales to retention and expansion. With all eyes on net revenue retention versus growth at all costs, Customer Success became a high priority. In addition, Product had to listen more closely for any friction points that might cause customers to churn and had to work harder to ensure that customers were able to achieve their desired outcomes.

Making the need for increased collaboration even more imperative is the nature of the digital experience itself. The fact that a digital customer experience is often embedded in the product creates a greater need to guide customers through the application in a more coherent and seamless manner. And that requires Product Management & Marketing (PMM), Product, Support, and CS teams to come together to coordinate their efforts and keep the lines of communication open.

Collaborating through a Digital CS Programs Team

Toward that end, one of the biggest recent shifts we've seen within SaaS companies is the creation of the dedicated digital team or dedicated Digital CS programs team (aka "scaled" team). Regardless of its name, the mission of this team is to single-mindedly focus on how to enhance retention and expansion through Digital Customer Success and scaled programs.

At Qualtrics, Kari Ardalan's digital and scale success team fills this role, serving as a shared service that brings departments together to outline the overall customer journey and determine what they can automate and/or digitize. The digital and scale success team sets company-wide digital success goals and develops broad strategies. Accomplishing these goals and strategies is the job of SteerCo, composed of leaders and representatives of the company's various functions (e.g., Professional Services, Support, Renewals).

Said Ardalan:

> The Qualtrics' process is to have a strategy council sit at the top with a business process owner, stakeholders, and a digital journey architect to outline the business pain points, process workflows, and operations. We then have a smaller "execution arm" composed of individuals who come back with solutions on how we will digitize and automate that workflow and test up until deployment. Finally, an Executive SteerCo, typically composed of C-suite-level executives from across the business, is in charge of reviewing all these efforts.

Ardalan stressed that at Qualtrics, the different cross-functional teams are not assigned to conduct discrete campaigns pegged to particular use cases or channels. Instead, they plan and execute initiatives that encompass large chunks of the customer journey.

> So when it comes to the renewal experience, we don't look at that in terms of singular campaigns, but at what the customer is experiencing across the board. We want to make it very coordinated.
>
> We started by meeting with business owners across the entire company. We outlined what all of the onboarding looked like and what all of the renewals looked like. We identified gaps in process flows and have been working to digitize them across the board.
>
> For every journey that we're looking to deploy, we have a business owner, and we have an executive sponsor, and we also have an execution arm of the [module] team. So I have a journey owner on my team who is part of the execution team. I also have a product manager. Together, they meet with the business owner and say, "Let's learn about your business. Where are the gaps? What can we digitize?"—and they have those meetings on a weekly cadence. And then, we have monthly SteerCos with the leadership, where we discuss all the decisions we made, what we're rolling out, and what's planned on the roadmap. So essentially, we have different gate reviews.

We recommend that SaaS companies—of every size and maturity level—organize and structure their cross-functional collaborations using the kind of model employed by Qualtrics. This is similar to the model we use at Gainsight to promote company-wide collaboration. Here, we established a Digital CS programs team with a dedicated leader (our Director of CX and Scale programs). Composed of individuals who work closely with key departments, the team functions as a central committee that sets company-wide CS goals, develops strategies, and recruits and oversees the subsidiary tiger teams. Each tiger team is tasked with collaborating on a particular digital initiative, and it frequently breaks into smaller execution teams to oversee deployment.

The Digital CS programs team might not be the group actually executing the initiatives, but they will be the ones listening for what's needed from each part of the organization and then bringing this input back to other Digital CS programs members. For example, if CS needs to do something within the product, Digital CS programs will first receive input from other parts of the organization regarding the proper content and cadence for the messaging, helping to effectively balance the priorities and needs of the customers and the other departments. Once the goals and strategies have been created, the appropriate tiger team can either execute the plan itself or determine which individuals should be responsible for execution. For instance, the person who owns in app might be tasked with executing new product release messages.

To staff your Digital CS programs team and tiger teams, look for people who can represent the different arms of your business. Someone from Product needs to be there, as well as representatives from CS, Marketing, and Sales. To recruit these reps, your Digital CS leader may want to approach senior management and say, "Hi, you've been identified as someone who has a stake in this team. Could you help with this or appoint a delegate?" Most likely, the C-Suite leader won't directly participate in the meetings but will delegate down. That's fine, but at least now the executive will have a finger on the pulse of the activities of the Digital CS programs.

The Elements of Effective Collaboration

Although the specifics of how cross-functional teams communicate and govern themselves will vary from company to company, we believe it's critical that every collaboration model be built around the following components:

- **A Limited Number of Joint Projects:** To keep your digital initiative focused on specific, tangible, and achievable objectives (and to avoid biting off more than you can chew), the teams should align around a limited number of projects. To start, for example, the teams could limit themselves to revising key One-to-Many Customer Communications, especially that all-important welcome email; and designing your digital approach to onboarding new users.
- **A Shared, Cross-Functional Framework Based on:**
  - *Finding Common Ground on What Everyone Needs to Do*: to provide customers with what they will need. For example: In the past, our Product Marketing team worked on what they knew was coming and what they needed to do. Meanwhile, CS worked on what they thought customers would need to be enabled. To establish common ground, we instituted a shared methodology called release impact sizing. Now all the features proposed for a release have a size assigned to them by the product manager and an SME (Subject Matter Expert) team, who determine the size based on customer impact (e.g., a big UI change for end users), as well as Go-to-Market implications. (Would the debut of this feature require a big marketing splash?) From there, every feature is graded from a quarterly release perspective, and the assigned scores determine both the launch strategy and the enablement assets to be delivered.
  - *Shared Project Milestones*. Create project milestones with cross-functional reviews and sign-offs. *Note:* It's important that the *scope* of the cross-functional reviews and sign-offs cover not only product and engineering readiness, but also your readiness to enable customers and properly market the release. Once the milestone and review processes are up and running, every member of the tiger team should feel enthusiastic about what's coming next. Why? Because once they hit every project milestone, they'll know they're fully prepared.
  - *A Shared Scorecard*. Finally, it's vital that you develop a shared scorecard to measure success. For example: With regard to release

process milestones, you might want to measure external *and* internal sentiment by soliciting answers to three core questions:

a. How prepared for the release did you feel?

b. What types of assets did you find most valuable?

c. How would you rate the quality of the release and all the new assets?

For certain initiatives, especially those that center on in-product guides and experiences, where the tiger team will likely comprise representatives from Product, CS, and Marketing, you will also want to determine who owns:

- **Tracking and Instrumentation:** This area typically should be owned by the Product or Product Operations team because it directly aligns with one of their key goals: to make data-driven product roadmap decisions. The Product team should track product usage to see how customers are using your product, identify friction points, see drop-offs in workflow completions, identify new feature adoption, and make usability improvements. How? The easiest way is to use an in-product analytics tool. This tool will make it simple to start instrumentation in a few clicks without any coding.

- **In-Product Experiences and Messaging:** Because your CSMs, marketers, and adoption specialists usually own customer experience and retention through other channels, it makes sense that they should craft the messages for in-product engagements. After all, they're set up to drive in-product journeys and they're capable of eliminating disjointed end user experiences. However, putting marketers in charge of in-product messaging isn't an absolute must. If using marketers doesn't make sense at your company, you may want to put another team in the driver's seat. Just make sure it's a team such as CS Operations, Product Operations, Education and Documentation, or other central teams that typically encourage product adoption. Depending on the size and maturity of your company, you may even want to consider forming a governance team. Companies such as Adobe and Dun & Bradstreet have robust governance teams to manage their in-app messaging.

- **Strategy and Approvals:** Strategy will depend heavily on your customer journeys and experiences. That's why partnering with

Customer Success teams will be critical in defining your strategy and pushing plans into action. Traditionally, the CS team works closest with the customer, and they have their fingers on pulse and health score data. This perfectly positions the CS team to define in-product adoption paths that feed off the right persona and customer segments.

Toward this end, one best practice for the CS team is focusing on each customer persona's "Role and Goal" to make more personalized recommendations. Thus, if a customer has the objective of "onboarding" in a particular product, you could walk them through the "ideal path"—in app—of how to set up that product for the "onboarding use case." This ideal path will vary, depending on the Role and Goal of each customer persona that you're addressing—admin, executive, front-line manager, salesperson, or others. For example, if I'm a Manager of Customer Success at Gainsight, my objective may be to "see my at-risk customers" or "build a dashboard to understand portfolio customer health." Therefore, *my* adoption happy path would be different from that of a CSM who's seeking upsell opportunities.

Another benefit of this approach is that it can help you better understand what your product's "stickiest features" are vis-à-vis the specific outcomes you're hoping to achieve. For example, an AI cheat sheet might not be as sticky or valuable to a CSM as it might be for an executive.

When it comes to approving in-product experiences, it makes sense to put the scale programs team in charge.

At Qualtrics, one challenge to developing a shared cross-functional framework was determining which metrics to use, as well as aligning behind who would own each metric, according to Kari Ardalan.

To simplify, we designed our metrics into three buckets: Reach, Quality, and Impact. Reach is like MAU/MAC for our customer portals or open rates; Quality is click-through rate on email or feature uptake rate based on completed calls to action or goal completion in our self-serve portals; and Impact is how you are impacting lagging outcomes like retention, expansion, and health scores.

If you're looking at self-serve portals, it's monthly active customers and are customers able to self-serve their entire goal—i.e., goal completion rates? So if we're sending a customer to our HUB to onboard, we want to make sure they complete that goal and hit certain onboarding milestones. We also built an engagement score so we could measure digital channels and . . . the health of a customer, and how they tie into retention and expansion. And then we studied the impact. Things we're looking at regarding impact are obviously retention and expansion rates. We are looking at NPS, as well, and then any cost savings or increases in productivity. We had our journey owners own that quality metric. How long are customers spending on these things? How are they interacting with our communications?

Meanwhile, the content team is more about deflection metrics—cost savings. And then, our Ops side of the house is more about reach. Are we able to touch the customers? Do we have monthly active users logging in, etc.? They are monitoring all those things.

The functional teams are then sharing these metrics. It's not one function saying, "We're going to go with this" and another saying, "We're going to go with that." We all agreed, in advance, on which leading indicators are most correlated with lagging indicators. We had to narrow them down because otherwise you get in this mode of measuring everything versus releasing new digital engagements and features.

In the nine months after Ardalan took charge of designing customer journeys across all channels, her team helped Qualtrics extend its reach from 30 percent of the customer base to more than 80 percent. (See Figure 9.1.) It also improved click-through rates to more than 30 percent,

And post-events and post-emails, we are seeing a 50 percent uptick in adoption of the [promoted] features, which is massive. You don't see that in many, many places.

Retention is lagging a little . . . so we're focused on onboarding. We had a retention rate of 85 percent for Year One customers, and we're trying to move that to above 90 percent. We just launched omnichannel self-serve onboarding, so we're paying close attention to see if that moves things up.

Back at Dealerware, the wealth of data supplied by Gainsight's product analytics and engagement platform helped to catalyze greater cross-functional collaboration across the company. "The consistent feedback through Gainsight organically created a biweekly product-quality meeting with Product and other teams," said Morgan Redwine, CS Ops and Strategy Manager. "We go through a range of topics, including bugs, NPS, and

Figure 9.1   Qualtrics' scoreboard/tracker.

churn reports. It's really cool, because everyone is taking an interest in Customer Success."[3]

Appoint a Dedicated Leader

In our experience, it is important that your Digital CS group and subgroups, whether you call them committees, teams, or modules, be headed by a dedicated leader, preferably someone who sits in a "neutral" department, such as Operations, or who's part of a dedicated Digital CS/Scaled team with a mission that includes determining who owns which metrics, who owns which parts of the digital life cycle, and who owns which digital experiences. Someone has to be the final arbiter of who owns what, as well as the entire customer journey, in order to create an experience that is seamless and pleasant rather than fragmented and frustrating. Someone has to be thinking, from start to finish, about how to avoid collisions between different departments.

You need a leader who can bring everyone together and say, "Okay, I understand that Product wants to do X, but Y is the metric that we're trying to drive." Your leader will need to work with the tiger teams to identify everything that needs to be accomplished and outline the precise steps that should be taken to ensure they are properly executed.

This is especially important if your organization has undertaken (or will soon undertake) an M&A. When you acquire a company, you want to be able to apply your playbook there so you don't create a disunited experience between product lines. After all, when you acquire another product line through an M&A, you introduce an entirely different Product team to your organization—one that doesn't know your processes, workflows, and culture. They're still operating in the ways they've always known, which you know nothing about. It's up to the Digital CS leader, therefore, to initiate conversations that will integrate all the Product teams.

As COO Jared Dunn said to CEO Richard Hendricks in HBO's *Silicon Valley* after their company (Pied Piper) acquired two start-up firms: "Richard, look out there. There's Optimoji and Sliceline T-shirts left and right. These are conquered soldiers still in their old uniforms. But we need everyone here to be Pied Pipers. I mean, you're asking them to spend the primes of their lives on your vision. Right? You need to go out there and lead them."

Is it important that your Digital CS (or scale programs) leader be seen as a neutral and impartial figure—someone whose background and experience makes them appear agnostic when it comes to the differing priorities and metrics of the various departments you work with?

In our experience, the leader's background and experience are less important than where the leadership role sits within the company. And we believe the *role* should sit within a neutral part of the organization. By doing this, you reduce the risk that the Digital CS programs leader will be seen as (consciously or unconsciously) favoring the interests and views of Product Marketing Manager (PMM) versus CS, or Sales versus Marketing.

At Gainsight, the role of director of CX and Digital CS programs sits in our CS Ops and Scale organization. Yes, the director supports the CS org, but she also works closely with functions such as Product, Marketing, and Sales. Because of where the role sits and her frequent interactions with different parts of the organization, she is regarded as a more neutral figure than she would be if her role were located in CS or Product. This works to our advantage every day and in countless situations.

For example, we take a hard line when it comes to advertising within the platform. If there is an event or experience that has an additional cost associated with it (such as tickets to our Pulse conference), we don't create in-app messages to promote it to customers. This isn't to say that Marketing doesn't *want* these promotions. But we've taken a hard line. We're willing to include free livestream events and save-the-date promotions in product, but not advertising that asks customers to buy something. No doubt, it's much easier for Marketing to stomach such a prohibition when it comes from the desk of a neutral leader than if it was dictated by someone widely seen as a CS or Product leader.

Getting Executive Buy-in

Getting the executive buy-in you'll need to staff your cross-functional teams can be tricky because you must be able to prove (or at least predict) the value that you will give back. You must be able to say, "By investing in a Digital/scaled team, here are the efficiency gains that we can expect."

At Gainsight, one metric we've used to justify the investment in our Digital CS team is *time saved*. We start by counting every email sent by the CS team, then apply a formula that assumes 10 minutes saved for each email that a CSM does *not* have to write. So if a CSM has 40 accounts and needs to send an email to their core contacts at each account (with two or three core contacts per account), substituting an automated email generated by a cross-functional team should save (using a conservative estimate) the CSM from having to send 80 emails. Using our formula, which assumes that each email requires 10 minutes to draft, this equals a total savings—for just one CSM—of 800 minutes.

At Qualtrics, Kari Ardalan's team uses a similar metric.

> We look at FTE (Full-Time Equivalent) savings. For frontline Support, we can easily measure [time savings] through ticket interactivity—how many tickets we deflect. But for Customer Success, we are looking at time spent. So . . . we try to find repeatable tasks and admin-related tasks that we can automate so we can directly correlate these with hours saved.

Building such formulas into your "Why staff my team?" arguments will go a long way toward making the case for headcount requests. Thus, as you consider ways in which you and your team can enhance different life cycle journeys, think in terms of time saved and/or revenues gained. For example, if you are designing a digital onboarding journey for new users, think in terms of how you're helping the end users by having just one CSM perform a particular activity across *all accounts*. Keep in mind, too, that once the new journey is set up, it can run in perpetuity. The time savings keep accruing—month upon month and year upon year.

Think, too, about your customers. How can you save *them* time? For example, consider one of your larger accounts—an account with a thousand end users. Your CSM cannot possibly know when each user signs in for the very first time. So how can the CSM ensure that new users receive the guidance on the platform that they need? Right now, the users are probably relying on their admins for this. So one of your team's goals could be eliminating that task from the admins' To-Do list by offering new users the training and guidance they need within the product itself. By doing so, you'll save your CSM time, you'll save the admin time, and you'll save the end users' time because now, instead of having to undergo off-platform training to understand how to use the product, they can learn how to use the product as they go—via in-app tutorials.

Share Your Results with *Everyone*

Do not hesitate to share the work of your cross-functional collaborations—and report the results of their initiative(s)—with everyone across the company. Everybody in your organization should have visibility into what users and customers are receiving and how they are responding.

Here's an example of how this works at Gainsight. Not long ago, our Digital CS programs team was charged with getting more G2 reviews from customers. The team knew that we had a lot of advocates. The question was: "How do we uncover them?" Eventually, the Digital CS programs team put together an in-app end user NPS survey, which targeted specific accounts and contained all the components of a closed-loop feedback program. With this done, they approached the marketing team and said, "This is what we're doing, and here's what our emails look like. Can you help us draft the follow-up emails?"

After this, the Digital CS programs team went to the CS team and said, "Here's what we're going to do on your behalf. Your names will not actually be on anything. You just need to know that this is happening. If accounts are coming up for renewal, and if there's a risk, this will provide a signal for you. But there's no action that you have to take on this." (We recently shifted this approach. Today, we are aggregating the results for the CSMs, alerting them to the key findings they should consider discussing with their customers.)

In sum, the Digital CS programs team developed the initiative, then collaborated with Marketing and CS (and also Product) to apprise them of their work and make sure they weren't doing anything that might interfere with what these teams were doing. The Digital CS programs team didn't necessarily hold meetings to say, "Here's what we're going to do to support a business goal around advocacy." In most cases, they simply shared their work asynchronously. Then, once the program was launched, they shared progress reports with the other teams. The initiative was launched on a Wednesday, and the Digital CS programs team reported back the following Tuesday with results.

This process allows members of every function to review a work in progress, as well as results, and say, "I have an issue with X," or "Y is causing some issues with our teams." So, if the end user NPS was likely to produce an increased workload for one team, we could make changes to prevent that. This is why we established quick, follow-up checkpoints. We want to make sure that after we launch something, especially if it's a cross-functional program, people can leverage those checkpoints to say, "Whoa! Stop!"

CS Technology and Data

As a leading maker of CS and CX solutions, we may be slightly biased when it comes to recommending specific products that you should purchase to execute your digital initiatives. Therefore, we will limit our suggestions to the kind of functionality you'll need at different stages of digital maturity.

If you are just embarking on your Digital CS journey, you will likely need a combination of three different functionalities—in addition to the platform(s) needed to store your data. At a minimum, you will need a platform that enables at least one of these channels:

- Email automation
- In-app communications
- Community and/or customer hub

You don't necessarily need all of these platforms, but you *will* need at least one.

To determine which product(s) to purchase, start by deciding how you want to communicate at scale. That's the first question to answer. "How will

I communicate at scale with my customers or share at scale with them?" You may also want to consider a webinar platform—whether it's Zoom, GoToMeeting, or something else—to enable additional one-to-many communications and record these webinars, which you can then add to other campaigns.

As you move toward the right side of the Digital Maturity Spectrum, you can more fully integrate the data on your different platforms. For example, you might start by sending a particular email communication and then expand the messaging to include the in-product channel and Community. Bit by bit, you start to intertwine the different solutions. As you grow toward the highest level of maturity, your aim is to create a single cohesive experience between your product, your emails, and the Community. You may even start dabbling in account-based Customer Success and account-based marketing.

Share Your Data

The first step in creating a smooth, consistent customer journey is simple: Focus on the customer. Remember, it's the customer's perspective that matters. Your number one goal across departments is to figure out why customers buy the things they buy, how they buy them, and how they use what they buy.

Use your data to acquire a more uniform vision of both the buying process and the customer's journey. Rather than looking at the buyer through the lens of your individual departments, you'll start seeing buying from the customer's viewpoint. From there, departments can determine how to use their unique strengths to improve that journey.

In addition, be sure to share metrics and responsibilities across different functions. In traditional models, responsibilities were dealt out by department, and, often, customer churn fell entirely on the shoulders of the CS team. However, to create a successful Digital CS program at scale, responsibilities must be spread across departments. If customer renewals are a high priority (as they should be), it makes sense that every department be asked to contribute to the success of this strategic initiative by undertaking the most relevant and impactful tasks. All departments need to share responsibility for customer churn. Maybe your Marketing team isn't communicating the right value to leads. Maybe Sales is overpromising. In all cases, sharing responsibility for churn and making it a cross-departmental cornerstone will bring your teams, and the customer experience, together.

Another way to prevent a siloed customer experience is to share customer profiles. These are the targets every department zooms in on. If they aren't perfectly aligned, you'll be delivering different experiences to the same user. For this reason, it's best that you install a single solution that everyone can rely on for customer data.

Again, your data doesn't have to be perfect on Day 1 of the digital journey. Start with the data you have, and use different tools to augment it. And one of the simplest ways to augment your data is to ask your customers to validate what you already have. Don't be afraid to enlist your customers' help. B2C companies do this all the time.

For example, our Digital CS leader has a ButcherBox subscription, which delivers meat to her doorstep once a month. Recently she received a short survey from the company asking about her preferences and interests: What types of recipes is she interested in? Is she just learning how to cook? Does she want to prepare restaurant-quality meals or simple meals with wholesome ingredients? We guarantee you that the next email she receives from ButcherBox will reflect all the answers she provided in that survey.

There's no good reason why your B2B company can't do something similar. Take inspiration from wherever you can get it. Don't feel as though you have to start from scratch or reinvent the wheel. Look to the B2C world—and elsewhere—for data collection and data augmentation models that you can adopt.

No Excuses

Many CS leaders and business leaders are under the impression that the prior recommendations for organizing people, processes, technology, and data are things that only larger SaaS organizations are capable of doing. Not true. In fact, the size and maturity of your organization doesn't matter. Many small organizations, including start-ups, are already figuring this out. And by figuring this out while you're still small, you will save your organization a great deal of money over the long term because you'll be able to scale and mitigate risk without having to hire an army of CS professionals.

In the wake of the recent tech downturn, every CEO reacted in one of two ways:

- "Let's go back to the old playbook. We'll sell our way through this!"
- "Let's lean into the future, recognizing that successful clients will drive our growth."

We recently heard that the CEO of a mid-size tech company had decided to solve the problem of super-low sales attainment (more than 70 percent of reps were missing their quotas) over the last few years by hiring more salespeople.

To each their own.

However, if you're really planning to sell your way to greater profitability, we would like to offer our help with a piece of technology well suited to the effort. Simply send us a stamped, self-addressed envelope (SASE) with the words "Sell your way through this" in the upper left-hand corner, and Nick will mail you his AOL dial-up CD ROM from 1999.

Summary

As more CS organizations incorporate digital technologies, use cases, and channels, existing problems often persist—and are sometimes magnified. That's because the only thing worse than a siloed CS organization is a siloed CS organization with digital superpowers. With their newfound ability to do more with less, CS teams are better positioned to "compete" with communications from Product, Marketing, and Support. The result? More spam in customer inboxes and more customer confusion wrought by dueling messages and scattered resources.

To prevent this, every team throughout the organization must start pulling in the same direction, at the same time.

We recommend that SaaS companies organize and structure cross-functional collaborations using the kind of model employed by Qualtrics and Gainsight. At Gainsight, we established a Digital CS programs team with a dedicated leader. Comprising representatives from key departments, it functions as a central committee that sets company-wide CS goals, develops strategies, and recruits and oversees subsidiary tiger teams. In turn, each tiger team is tasked with collaborating on a particular digital initiative, and these teams frequently break into smaller execution teams to oversee deployment. At both Qualtrics and Gainsight, this model has proven highly effective in driving organization-wide efficiencies and a better customer experience.

Although the specifics of how the cross-functional teams communicate and govern themselves will vary from company to company, we believe it's critical that every tiger team program be built around the following components:

- A limited number of joint projects
- A shared, cross-functional framework based on shared project milestones
- A shared scorecard that covers tracking and instrumentation, in-product experiences and messaging, and strategy and approvals

It is important that your Digital CS group and subgroups be headed by a dedicated leader, preferably someone who sits in a neutral department, such as CS Operations. You will need a dedicated leader to determine, among other things, who owns which metrics, who owns which parts of the digital life cycle, and who owns which digital experiences.

Getting executive buy-in for headcount, along with the support you need for your cross-functional teams, can be tricky. At Gainsight, one metric we've used to justify the headcounts for our cross-functional teams is *time saved*. At Qualtrics, Kari Ardalan's team looks at FTE savings.

Once everyone on a cross-functional team, and at the executive level, has reviewed a particular initiative, do not hesitate to share that work—and report the results of the initiative—with everyone across the company. Everybody in your organization should have visibility into what users and customers are receiving and how they are responding.

If you are just embarking on your Digital CS journey, you will likely need a combination of three different functionalities—in addition to the platform(s) needed to store your data. At a minimum, you will need a platform that enables at least one of these channels: email automation, in-app communications, and Community and/or customer hub.

Use your data to acquire a more uniform vision of both the buying process and the customer's journey. Rather than looking at the buyer through the lens of your individual departments, you'll start seeing buying from the customer's viewpoint. From there, departments can determine how to use their unique strengths to improve that journey.

Your data doesn't have to be perfect on Day 1. Start with the data you have, and use different tools to augment it. One of the simplest ways to augment your data is to ask your customers to validate what you already have. Don't be afraid to enlist your customers' help.

10

Optimizing Your Digital Toolkit

Checklist

When it comes to your Community and/or Customer Hub:

- Determine your goals and priorities and then map them to Community use cases.
- Remember: Too much of a good thing can produce a disjointed CX.
- Know your audience and key personas.
- "Prime the pump" by posting questions and content to Community that piques users' interest, especially in the first weeks/months after you launch the platform.
- Encourage conversations and post content that reflect your organization's culture and values.
- Examine your company's broader ecosystem of tools, channels, and touchpoints to help determine the unique purpose and strategy of your Community.
- Compile your learnings into a Community strategy and action plan using the Objective, Goals, Strategies, and Measures (OGSM) framework.

- Strive to develop face-to-face conversations between individual users and cohorts, especially during the early months following your Community launch.
- Consider driving prospects and at-risk customers to Community.

When it comes to automated email and in-app messaging:

- Design messaging campaigns for each stage of the customer life cycle—for example, campaigns relevant to onboarding, deeper adoption, renewals, and others.
- Target specific personas and users with messages that speak to their situations and needs as well as their product usage.
- Establish checkpoints in your digital communications so you can evaluate and adjust your messaging based on any risk factors that have surfaced with that customer.
- When you send automated emails, be sure there is a person on the other end of those emails who's available to respond to customer inquiries.
- When choosing channels, consider the persona and life cycle moment of the user.
- Target your messaging based on usage, behavior, and health data.
- Throttle to avoid spamming customers.
- Employ a Knowledge Center bot to keep users from having to leave the product.
- Avoid interrupting key workflows with in-app messages.
- Avoid blatantly self-serving communications.
- View email and in-app in tandem.

Even the best digital solutions will have limited value if you're unable to effectively harness them to accomplish more with less while improving the customer experience. Given how often we hear about disjointed customer journeys and siloed communications campaigns, as well as client complaints about being spammed by vendors, we've devoted this chapter to a discussion of best digital communications practices, along with a few bad practices, which we've collected from discussions with our customers and other

Subject Matter Experts (SMEs). Although the list of tips and best practices is not exhaustive, it does answer many FAQs that we receive regarding communities and customer hubs, email campaigns, and in-app messaging.

Community/Customer Hub

When it comes to Community and customer hub, it's important to do the following.

Determine Your Goals and Priorities and Then Map Them to Community Use Cases

A Community needs to serve a purpose, and that purpose can ultimately touch on a number of different Community use cases. See Figure 10.1 for the five most common use cases, along with their related metrics and activities.

When building a Community in the B2B SaaS space, we recommend that you consider all the use cases shown. Eventually, they are all likely to prove valuable. As with any digital initiative, however, it's best not to tackle everything at once. Instead, consider what your primary business problems and opportunities are, then map those problems and opportunities to these use cases to determine the Community's main focus. For instance, if you urgently need to scale your Support organization and improve the product feedback loop to drive more product adoption and satisfaction, this would be a good (and very common) starting point. You could focus your efforts here during the first few months and increase the likelihood of achieving early successes.

When Gainsight launched its Community 10 years ago, we initially focused on providing users with a simple Q&A forum, with a view toward ticket deflection. However, as more admins began visiting our Community, the focus widened to include product-idea posts and discussions. Soon the product-idea-and-update use case became so ingrained that whenever our CSMs heard a customer say, "Hey, we could really use this feature," they felt comfortable telling them to post their ideas on Community. Our Community continues to be an active place for posting new product and feature ideas, but we have expanded the number of channels that visitors can access within Community, increased the platform's appeal to a more diverse set of personas, and encouraged a broader range of discussion topics and SME

	Service and P2P Support	Education and Inspiration	Advocacy	Networking and Connection	Product Ideas and Updates
Modules	Community Knowledge Base	Community Knowledge Base Events	Conversations Groups Events	Groups Events	Ideas Product Updates
Metrics	Self-service ratio, deflection, answers by peer	Content helpfulness, event attendance and survey feedback	Event attendance, Group membership and participation	Event attendance and survey feedback, Group membership and participation	Ideas and votes, ideas and votes delivered
Activities and Focus	Moderation, Gamification, KB content, superuser engagement KB content (articles), webinars,	KB content (articles), webinars, guest contributors	Webinars, events and group facilitation	Event attendance and survey feedback, Group membership and participation	Idea follow-ups, publishing Product Updates
Supporting platforms	Support portal, video hosting platform	Video hosting platform, webinar platform, LMS	Advocacy and incentives platform, webinar platform	Webinar platform	Roadmap platform

Figure 10.1   We recommend that you consider all five use cases shown. Just don't try to tackle them all at once.

thought leadership posts, including inspiration-level conversations around Digital Customer Success. Today, our Community/customer hub averages 12,000 visitors a month—250 to 300 of whom are posting each month.

Too Much of a Good Thing Can Produce a Disjointed CX

As your Community expands to reflect your growing list of goals and priorities, closely monitor the customer experience to ensure it doesn't deteriorate. When they first launch Communities, companies tend to be relatively small and have fairly simple products. As they grow and their products become more complex, some companies allow their communities to grow into multiheaded hydras. These firms start adding more content and more tools. They add more blogs and white papers and YouTube videos. Before long, the Community becomes a de facto customer hub that's so hard to navigate that it's impossible for customers to quickly find answers. The content and tools may be great, but unless the teams in charge of the tools and content devise ways to unify and tailor the customer experience and (if need be) upgrade the search capabilities, visitors often will be stymied in their quests for information. And that defeats the whole purpose of providing them with either a simple Community *or* a customer hub.

Know Your Audience and Key Personas

Having determined where you want to focus your initial Community efforts, it's a good idea to reflect on the nature of your audience. Most likely, your company has already defined the key personas that comprise your audience, so you can start there. After that, ask yourself three simple questions:

1. What is the size of your audience and what are the key personas?
2. What kind of relationship does each audience segment have with your product?
3. What are their biggest needs and challenges related to your product?

Each question should offer insight into the unique situation you're in and what kind of Community strategy will work for you. For example, the size of your audience will tell you something about how easy it will be to achieve critical mass and organic growth in terms of ongoing engagement. If you have only 100 or 200 customers in total, with perhaps one or two active users of your product per company, your strategy will need to include consistent proactive efforts to engage this audience. Similarly, the nature of customers' relationships with your product will also inform your strategy. If your customers spend an hour or two per week engaging with your product, you will be in a very different position than if customers work with your product all day, every day.

The third question about what your customers need is probably the most essential. It seems an obvious consideration, but it's very often missed. To get a Community strategy right, you need to know what your audience needs and wants most. Do they have a lot of technical challenges? Are they mostly running into how-to questions and seeking best practices? Do they have a lot of product ideas? Are they looking to network and develop their careers? What you want to do with the Community has to match the needs of your audience. Failing to thoroughly examine audience needs is why some Community teams are surprised when they end up with a support-focused Community when that wasn't their goal. In the end, your customers will show you with their behavior what they want and expect from the Community.

To gain a deeper understanding of your audience, it's also a good idea to peruse your data for insights. For example, what are the top 10 FAQs received by the Support team? What are the main reasons for churn? What are the top success factors? What are the biggest challenges that the Customer Success team runs into with their customers? One of the most powerful things you can do, if you're able, is arrange some customer interviews. This will provide deep insights that you can apply to your Community strategy in terms of where to focus your content creation and engagement as well as where the most effort will be needed to meet your audiences' needs.

Prime the Pump

"If you build it, they will come" may be good advice for luring the ghosts of celebrated baseball players to the diamond you're building in a cornfield, but it's unlikely to attract visitors to your Community—and if it does, they may not stay long. Not unless you give them a reason to visit—again and again—by posting questions and other content that routinely piques their interest. If you're not sure which topics will generate a lot of interest, don't be afraid to simply ask your Community members. "What would you like to see? What do you expect? What would make your visits more worthwhile?" Reach out to your Community and literally ask those questions. That's always a good start.

Another approach is to examine the content that your Community members are already using most. Are they using webinars? If so, consider aggregating all your webinars in one centralized location. Are they reading blog posts and articles? Collect these into a central repository on the platform. In sum, start with the content you already have. You don't have to start by creating something completely new and different.

In the first few weeks or months after launching the Community, you will probably need to prime the pump by having your Community manager, moderators, and even your CSMs post content that sparks animated discussions and serves as templates for the types of discussions you'd like customers to start posting themselves. After all, creating an engaged and self-sustaining Community means encouraging customers to post their own questions and content. So start by posting topics that, based on your understanding of the customers, are likely to spark lively discussions and debates. Steer the content and conversations in directions that are interesting for people. Eventually, you should reach a point where customer-generated topics will make up the bulk of your platform's conversations, but in the early stages of Community maturity, you will probably need to spark those conversations proactively.

And when we say "conversation," we're referring to everything from conversation-starter questions generated by your thought-leadership articles to video profiles and webinars created by Community members. As soon as feasible, you want to be able to say to some customers, "You seem very active as a Community member—someone who's doing and saying some very interesting things. Would you be interested in posting a blog post around the Digital Customer Success initiatives with which you'd had success? Or would you be interested in a Q&A profile of you and your company?" Aim for something less than a polished webinar that your marketing team might prepare, but more sophisticated and engaging than a one-time post.

Devise ideas for content in which the Community would be interested by connecting the dots between what customers need/want and which Community members could serve as content-generating SMEs willing to share their stories and expertise.

To determine how to start good conversations, we've found it helpful to collaborate with Product Marketing and the CS team to give us a sense of "This is what customers and prospects want to talk about." In this respect, your Community manager will serve as a broadcast news producer—someone with their finger on the pulse of what the audience wants. Someone who then books SMEs as webinar or podcast guests or as content creators.

Sometimes your Community team will be like talk show hosts, prepping interviewees to appear on their programs. At other times, the team will be actively seeking out, and recruiting, customers to lead roundtable discussions or to create two-minute videos about use cases that worked especially well for them. There are a thousand different things you can do to generate conversations and content that will contribute to the Knowledge Center on your platform.

Reflect Your Culture and Values

Once you decide where you want to focus your efforts and have validated that you understand your audience and their needs, consider another factor that is sometimes ignored—your company's culture and values.

Here are a few questions to get you started with this:

- How risk-averse is your organization?
- Are you allowed to experiment or do you need to prove value quickly?
- How does your organization look at value?

The Community strategy that works best for you will be one that's dialed in to your organization's unique culture. If your company is highly risk-averse, you will likely need a methodical plan that carefully progresses through measured incremental steps. On the opposite side of the spectrum, you might find that the best strategy requires you to be bold, move fast, and experiment, seeing every failure as a lesson to embrace. There is no right or wrong answer here. It all depends on your culture and what will resonate.

It's also a good idea to reflect on how your organization talks about value. Do you need to produce a robust ROI model that demonstrates clear financial gains or cost savings? Or does your leadership team and the wider organization understand the intrinsic value of Community engagement and respond better to storytelling and demonstrations of customer intimacy? These nuances can inform how you think about your metrics and KPIs.

Although Community can be a very powerful CS tool, it tends to be a slow build. Unfortunately, many SaaS leaders have trouble wrapping their heads around this paradox because they don't like slow builds. They want to see immediate business value, so you need to arm yourself with business value stories that you can present to senior management. As soon as you can celebrate any wins, take these to the executive team. "We're already seeing activity X, which will eventually support Goal Y, which will ultimately produce business value Z."

For example, in our Community's beginner admins group, we have a group champion who's been posting a crossword puzzle of Gainsight terminology for the past several months. A few people would comment on the puzzle, which was great, but it wasn't until recently that a member of this group posted an actual question. This represents a small win vis-à-vis enhanced engagement. It was something that happened organically, but it took time. So celebrate small wins as they happen and connect the dots to the business value they will generate down the road.

Examine Your Ecosystem

Your Community doesn't exist in a vacuum. It's going to be part of a broader ecosystem of tools, channels, and touchpoints. The nature of this overall ecosystem is something you should take into account to determine the unique purpose and strategy of your Community. To get started, here are three questions to ask:

1. What other resources does your audience have access to, and where do they engage with each other today?
2. How will you position your Community in the ecosystem?
3. What is the unique purpose of your Community within this ecosystem?

After considering the needs of your audience, you also need to consider what other touchpoints might be fulfilling those needs today—touchpoints that may be competing with the goals you've established for your Community. For example, it's possible that your audience has a strong inclination for networking, and they are already meeting this need via LinkedIn or Slack. In this case, your next step might be considering whether networking should be a primary focus of your Community. To successfully adopt this use case as part of your Community program, you would need to ensure that you're offering something that is lower effort than what already exists—or something that adds value. (Otherwise, this use case will not gain traction.) For example, your Community could host unique groups and events to facilitate networking that doesn't exist anywhere else. To take things further, however, you may need to consider ways of tapping into your other touchpoints to establish connections and cross-links to the Community.

These questions will help you determine what purposes your Community is going to fulfill that aren't being (entirely) fulfilled somewhere else. This is important to the long-term success of your Community because members will come back to a Community that has a clear purpose—one that's meeting a need that isn't being satisfied elsewhere.

Compile Your Learnings into a Community Strategy and Action Plan

One of our favorite ways of summarizing a Community strategy, especially when creating a plan for a full year or longer—is using the OGSM framework. For shorter time frames, such as quarters, the Objectives and Key Results (OKR) framework can be more useful. There are many resources online about how to work with OGSM, so we won't go deeply into the methodology, but the essence is quite simple: Compile your OGSM into a clear, one-page overview.

A simple template for a Community plan that uses the OGSM framework, including examples of common strategic themes, follows. One level lower you would also have a set of specific tactics (with timelines) tied to each of the strategies. Collectively, these would make up your complete plan and roadmap. Make sure to tie your plan to a set of concrete actions and tactics with timelines and owners.

Objective: Your Community objective for this time frame in one sentence	
Goals and Measures	**Strategies**
Your first goal and KPIs, e.g., around **support and self-service**	Your first strategy, e.g., around the **positioning of the Community and promotion**
Your second goal and KPIs, e.g., around **engagement and advocacy**	Your second strategy, e.g., around **content planning and creation**
Your third goal and KPIs, e.g., around **product feedback**	Your third strategy, e.g., around **driving engagement and advocacy**
	Your fourth strategy, e.g., around **data and insights**
	Your fifth strategy, e.g., around **optimizing your platform and integrations**

Strive to Develop Human Connections

Especially during the early months following your Community launch, strive to develop face-to-face conversations between individual users and cohorts. Early on, we recognized that an off-platform group of customer admins, who were meeting on Slack, became such an instant success because it started as a virtual meetup. The people in the group felt like they were interacting with real humans just like themselves. This promoted feelings of validation: "These are people just like me, who share the same challenges, so I feel very comfortable talking with them." This dynamic is something that develops much more readily through face-to-face interactions, but it's also a dynamic that is harder—and more time-consuming—to build. Of course, that is the nature of human connections. They require the kind of trust that only develops with the passage of time.

So when you're just starting to create this new space that you call Community, feel free to gather a few people together for a video conference call. (You may even want to do this before you actually launch the platform because you don't want to launch the space and then discover that it's empty. You don't want to email thousands of customers and say "Come to this space," but when they arrive, there's nothing happening.) Start by connecting visitors with each other—even if you have to do it off the platform. Give your first visitors a chance to engage in face-to-face interactions. In this way, you can learn what they most want to talk about. From there, some of these early adopters will become the pilot members of your Community space. They will begin generating questions and other content, so that when other visitors arrive, they'll get the sense that they've entered a vibrant space populated by other customers like them. In other words, they'll arrive at a party that's already in full swing rather than an empty ballroom.

We live in an age when many people look to software to establish human connections. "I need human connections, so I'll buy Zoom or become active on social media." Although these tools can help to facilitate human connections, they cannot create those connections in the first place. Even today, it takes human beings to establish human relationships, so when you're launching a Community, don't make the mistake of viewing human interactions as a software fix. Making such connections is a very human problem that requires human beings to solve. At best, software solutions can assist, but they cannot create and sustain human interactions if there are no humans present on the Community platform.

Consider Driving Prospects and At-Risk Customers to Community

Many SaaS businesses are focused on driving customers to their communities/customer hubs to digitize onboarding, adoption, and new feature announcements. This focus is good, but why limit yourself to these use cases? In our experience, there is no customer life cycle moment in which a Community/customer hub cannot play a useful role. For example, if a prospective customer asks to talk with a reference, why not connect that prospect with the advocates who are active in your Community? The same holds true when existing customers are at risk of churning. We've learned that it can be very beneficial to introduce dissatisfied customers to customer advocates in the Community, especially if those advocates once had similar complaints or underwent similar challenges. Consider novel ways to expand the number of use cases for your Community and customer hub.

Automated Email and In-App Messaging

Today's consumers expect a personalized experience from every product, whether it's a B2C or B2B solution. In CS, personalization means distributing the right content to the right users at the precise moment that they need the information. (See Figure 10.2.) To help you facilitate this goal, let's start by looking at three "must practices," before moving to a discussion of best practices:

1. *Design messaging campaigns for each stage of the customer life cycle*—for example, campaigns relevant to onboarding, deeper adoption, renewals, and others. Whether your content is delivered via email or in app, make sure it aligns to the user's journey stage. That means sending content relevant to the adoption phase for users in the adoption phase and content relevant to the onboarding stage for new users. If your product has a free trial, you'll want to communicate a different set of recommended actions to these users than you would to fully onboarded premium users.

2. *Target specific personas and users with messages that speak to their specific situations and needs as well as their product usage.* One of the worst sins a communications campaign can commit is distributing messages that are irrelevant to the user type. If you're sending someone content that's designed to persuade them to activate features to which they don't have access (because they're not an admin), that is a profoundly negative experience. Always make sure your message is relevant and timely.

3. *Establish checkpoints in your digital communications* so you can evaluate and adjust your messaging based on any risk factors that have surfaced with that customer. For example, if a renewal is coming up, but the customer hasn't completed certain feature activation steps, you'll want to adjust your messaging to avoid appearing tone deaf.

CS Journey Automation

This all boils down to recognizing that different user types need different message types at different times. For instance, the channels and messages adopted for admin users should be different than those targeting new users (who are typically onboarded after the admins). It's all about creating and fine-tuning the channels and messages you're adopting for different users at different points in their journeys based on their specific needs. (See Figure 10.2.)

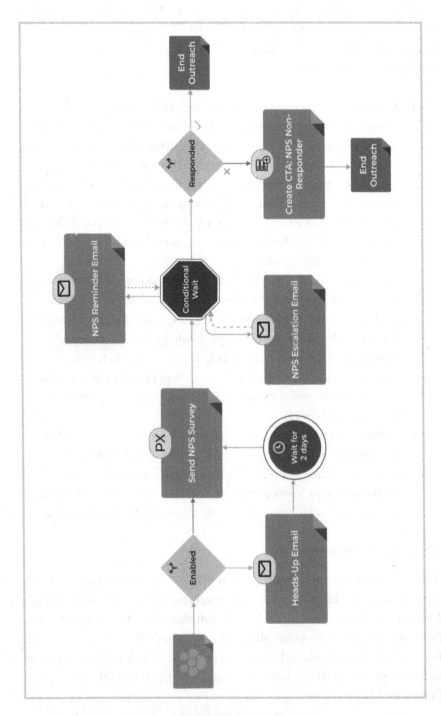

Figure 10.2   Example of an automated CS journey playbook.

Some best practices to help you personalize the digital customer experience are discussed next.

Amplify Human Voices

When you send automated emails, be sure there is a person on the other end of those emails with a name and face—someone who's available to respond to customer inquiries whenever necessary. This doesn't have to be a single individual in CS or Support. You can assign several people to handle queries via a shared inbox, as long as *someone* can reach out to users. The same holds true for in-app content. If you're sending something in app, especially when you're touting a video or webinar that features named speakers or has a particular touchpoint, it's always a good idea to put a name and face to these automated digital media to humanize the experience as much as possible.

When Choosing Channels, Consider the Persona and Life Cycle Moment of the User

Which channels should you choose for a particular communications campaign? To a large extent, that will depend on the personas you wish to reach and where they are in the customer life cycle. For example, email tends to be the better choice for reaching decision makers who spend relatively little time within the product on a day-to-day basis, whereas in-app messages are best for admins and standard users (as well as superusers) who are continuously in the product.

Your decision should also be based, in part, on user behavior and health. For instance, email makes the most sense for a reengagement campaign because users who need to be reengaged are (by definition) not using the product. Therefore, you aren't going to reach these people by sending them in-app messages. For the same reason, email is also a good choice for onboarding because new users aren't necessarily using your product very much (if at all). As new users grow accustomed to the product, however, it makes sense to then shift your messages toward in app—again, depending on the persona. (See Figure for 10.3 for examples.)

Target Your Messaging Based on Usage, Behavior, and Health Data

Determine which messages and cadences to use with particular users based not only on their personas, but also on their usage, behavior, and current health. For example, when you're sending a message to someone about activating a feature, you wouldn't want to send them activation instructions if they've already activated that feature. You also wouldn't want to send them information about activating a deeper feature if they're displaying poor usage of a more basic, but functionally important, feature in your product.

This practice is about examining usage data to do more than say "They've checked this box, so let's move on," but to make sure that whenever you send automated emails or in-app messages, they take account of the recipient's usage and health, as well as their persona and their individual journey. In order to get granular with your digital messages, consider when users were last seen, how often they're working in the product, and any significant trends or patterns that you can detect regarding their usage and behavior.

Obviously, you'll need to have sufficient adoption data to help you understand and segment your audience well enough to send the right messages at the right time. Otherwise, if you're merely targeting based on persona information around who a user is, that data may be totally irrelevant to how they're actually using your product. It won't tell you if someone is struggling. It won't tell you whether someone is a superuser or a key stakeholder.

Throttle to Avoid Spamming Customers

To keep from bombarding individual customers and particular audience segments with unwanted emails and in-product messages, adopt a practice known as throttling. In the automotive world, a throttle is a device that controls the flow of fuel to an engine. In Digital CS, the throttle controls the flow of messages to the recipient. From the standpoint of product experience, throttling enables you to limit how many total engagements a user will see within a specific time frame. It lets you make sure that you're only surfacing the most relevant messages first and to set priorities for the different types of messages being sent. For example: Whereas you'd probably want to assign a high priority to a system outage report because this news is something every user should know, content related to a deeper adoption campaign is probably a lower priority and, as such, not something that should be sent to every user.

With a product such as Gainsight product analytics and engagement platform, you can adjust your throttling to make sure you're always sending the most relevant messages, and you can also set limits on how many total messages specific recipients will receive within a specific time frame. The limits will be based not only on the time frame but also on who the user is. From there, you can fine-tune your frequencies and total number of communications to ensure that you're not spamming any one audience segment or customers in general. Set your throttling parameters based on what you know about a particular persona rather than merely guessing. Initially, of course, there may be some trial and error involved until you're able to iterate to the optimum experience. The parameters will also vary based on the type of persona you're contacting and what types of messages you're sending in app or via email.

For these reasons, we recommend that you start small, examine the results, and expand the program only after you determine the frequencies and totals that produce the optimum results. Keep your eye on the data to learn when your messages are actually moving the needle when it comes to onboarding or when they're actually encouraging people to use the features you want them to use. Leverage the data to continually refine how many times you reach out with a particular message. Determine if that message is generating results that are better or worse in terms of achieving your adoption or retention goals.

Employ a Knowledge Center Bot to Keep Users from Having to Leave the Product

Also known as Help bots and Support bots, these in-app bots allow you to aggregate all your Community content, in-app guides, and other resources in a single place so users can access the information quickly and easily, without ever having to leave the product. Since the goal of every CS organization is to convince as many customers as possible to adopt the product, especially the golden features, once you've succeeded in getting people into the product, it's a good idea to keep them there rather than forcing them to look outside for any resources they need to consult. Integrating these resources into the product is also part of a smart omnichannel strategy in terms of making the customer experience, including any touchpoints, a more cohesive one.

At Gainsight, our Knowledge Center bot is an embedded widget that appears in all our products. Among other things, the bot can push users to adopt certain features and can instantly access key guides and other resources, giving customers the opportunity to surface—in app—all the conversations that are occurring in their Community forums.

So, if one of your customers has a question, they can search for an answer from the main tab, and your Knowledge bot will conduct a search of all your resources—all your in-app articles and Community content. Even with this setup as it is today, our Knowledge Center bot makes it very easy for your customers to find the information they need without having to leave the product.

From a user standpoint, the chief benefit of a Knowledge bot is not having to leave the product to visit the Community, find their content, and then risk becoming distracted. From your vantage point, the chief benefit of the bot is keeping your users where they are, so they can continue to get value from your product.

Avoid Interrupting Key Workflows with In-App Messages

If you're old enough to remember Mr. Paperclip (aka "Clippy"), the animated virtual assistant who appeared in Microsoft Office solutions from the mid-1990s until the mid-2000s, then you know just how exasperating it can be when your work is interrupted by in-product messages and virtual assistants. As you may recall, Clippy was wont to suddenly materialize while you were in the midst of writing memos and letters, bringing your workflow to a screeching halt with a cheerful "It looks like you're writing a letter. Can I help?" Initially, Clippy may have been welcomed by a few first-time Microsoft Office users, but for the most part, his interruptions were infuriating. Our advice, therefore, is that you *not* follow in the footsteps of dear old Clippy.

When designing in-app messages to persuade users to adopt a new feature, or when you simply want to communicate a morsel of news, the best practice is to avoid interrupting key workflows. You never want to surface a message while users are in the middle of trying to complete an action. And, depending on how your information is displayed in product, it may also make sense not to share messages on certain pages. (Keep your user interface in mind when determining where it makes sense to display in-product messages.)

There are also best practices around how different types of content should be displayed. For example, if your message is critical—"We really need you to adopt this feature"—the content might appear as a full screen overlay, with dialog appearing in the very center of the screen. In contrast, if the information is merely nice to know, it may be better to opt for a "tool tip" location or a "hot spot"—those little bubbles that appear in a corner of the screen.

Be judicious in where you display your in-app messages. Consider whether a particular message deserves to be front and center in the product, or whether it should appear on the periphery, allowing users to take deeper dives only if they're interested in learning more. (For more information on best practices for in-app messages, visit the resources section of the Gainsight website: https://www.gainsight.com/resources/.)

Avoid Blatantly Self-Serving Communications

Obviously, many (if not all) of your customer communications are undertaken out of self-interest—spurring adoption, renewals, upsells, and the like. But your communications should also keep customers, and their interests, in mind. Too often, businesses send communications that are blatantly self-serving because they're trying to accomplish a business goal or drive a business outcome without ever thinking "What's in it for the customer?" or "How will this communication help the customer?" Failing to make communications customer-centric is one of the worst practices that we see. So instead of thinking "We need to drive this renewal process," flip that viewpoint around to "How will this message be perceived by the customer? How can we make the message helpful to them?"

Case in point: When you're pushing users to value through in-app messages (or email), certain product features tend to translate to higher retention and adoption rates. Use of these golden features usually translates into higher retention because the customers are getting more value from your product when they utilize them. One of the best practices around golden features is driving customers to adopt them in order to maximize the likelihood of successful outcomes and minimize Time to Value (TTV). Conversely, one of the worst practices that we see is doing the opposite—pushing customers to adopt features from which they'll derive little or no value or because the adoption of those features is statistically more likely to generate an upsell. Not all features are created equal, and not all customers are created equal. It should be your mission to send communications that guide specific customers to the specific features that are most likely to enable *their* success, not the features that are most likely to improve your bottom line in the short term.

View Email and In App in Tandem

For the sake of clarity, we sometimes break down our suggestions regarding automated emails and in-app messaging by channel. However, another best practice is to treat the two channels as a single communications entity rather than two siloed entities. In other words, as you plan your communication initiatives, think of these two media channels as working in tandem. After all, in order to create communications that are properly segmented by customer and persona, as well as ones that are timely and value-adding, you often will need to employ both channels simultaneously or sequentially.

For example, you might use email to drive new users into the application, but once they go into the product, this will trigger an in-app message that tries to persuade them to adopt a specific feature that's likely to provide a lot of value. So avoid thinking in terms of email versus in app, and instead think in terms of which channels (individually and collectively) are most likely to generate the customer behavior that will benefit them—and you—the most.

Finally, as you think about the entire customer journey and how to orchestrate email with in-app communications with Community and/or the customer hub, keep in mind that it's okay to start small. For example, you might want to start (as we did) by automating a single email associated with the onboarding process. It's a great idea to start with that one email and then automate two to three additional email types as you learn and grow. Or you could start with email as a channel and then add in-app messaging as a supplement as you continue to grow the email program.

Look for opportunities to iterate based on your learnings—once you've acquired some useful data on what's working best and what people are actually engaging with. Rather than letting the fear of getting started block your path to Digital CS, start with a small project, then grow your other channels when you're ready.

Summary

Even the best digital solutions will have limited value if you're unable to effectively harness them to accomplish more with less while improving the customer experience. Given how often we hear about disjointed customer journeys and siloed communications campaigns, as well as client complaints about being spammed by vendors, we've devoted this chapter to a discussion of best digital communications practices regarding your Community and customer hub as well as in-app messaging and automated email.

When it comes to Community and customer hub, it's important to:

- Determine your goals and priorities and then map them to Community use cases.
- Continually monitor the customer experience to ensure it doesn't deteriorate.
- Know your audience and key personas.
- Prime the pump, at least in the beginning, by posting questions and other content that routinely piques users' interest.
- Reflect your company's culture and values.
- Examine your entire communications ecosystem.
- Compile your learnings into a Community strategy and action plan.
- Strive to develop human connections.
- Consider driving prospects and at-risk customers to Community.

When it comes to automated email and in-app messaging, best practices include:

- Designing messaging campaigns for each stage of the customer life cycle.
- Targeting specific personas and users with messages that speak to their specific situations and needs, as well as their product usage.
- Establishing checkpoints in your digital communications so you can evaluate and adjust your messaging based on any risk factors that have surfaced with that customer.

Some best practices include:

- Amplifying human voices.
- Considering the persona and life cycle moment of the user when determining which channels to use.
- Targeting your messaging based on usage, behavior, and health data.
- Throttling to avoid spamming customers.
- Employing a Knowledge Center bot to keep users from having to leave the product.

- Avoiding interruptions to key workflows with in-app messages.
- Avoiding blatantly self-serving communications.
- Viewing email and in app in tandem.

As you think about the entire customer journey and how to orchestrate email with in-app communications with Community and/or the customer hub, keep in mind that it's okay to start small. Rather than letting the fear of getting started block your path to Digital CS, start with a small project, then grow your other channels when you're ready.

11

The Ability to Be More Human

Digital CS Is About Building Customer Loyalty

Ultimately, Customer Success is about building loyalty among your customer. As Nick wrote in the book *Customer Success*, the general consensus is that there are two types of customer loyalty: attitudinal loyalty and behavioral loyalty, also known as emotional loyalty and intellectual loyalty. The premise is that there are customers who are loyal because they have to be—because your product is the only game in town, far less expensive, or much more convenient—and there are customers who are loyal because they *love* your brand and your product(s).[1]

As a SaaS vendor, attitudinal loyalty is preferable for a variety of reasons. Among other things, attitudinally loyal customers are often willing to pay a higher price, are less vulnerable to competition, and are more likely to advocate for your brand. They are also more likely to remain your customers and buy more stuff from you. Unfortunately, attitudinal loyalty is also much harder to establish and sustain because it's expensive. It's expensive to build products that customers really love instead of products they merely own. It's expensive to create an experience that continually delights instead of an experience that simply tries not to annoy.

197

But if, as Summer suggested, attitudinal loyalty can be created and sustained by delivering not just the occasional Big Moment of surprise and delight but by continually delivering small, pleasant experiences to customers over the course of the relationship, then Digital CS, more than ever, is foundational to the creation of a positive customer experience. (To learn more about Big Moments, read Chip and Dan Heath's groundbreaking book *The Power of Moments*.[2])

And, in turn, a positive customer experience is foundational to the retention and expansion of your customer base. After all, those magical moments (big and small) are not created by machines, but by humans—by employees across your organization. And as we've mentioned time and again, Digital CS is not designed to replace human interactions with customers but to enhance them by freeing your people to engage in more intimate, higher-value interactions with all your clients, not just the largest ones.

Many of you were aware of this fact before you opened this book, which reflects just how far Customer Success has come over the past 10 years. Back then, the early charter for many CS organizations could be summarized as "Okay, we have this new Customer Success team. Let's turn them loose to fix everything related to churn and retention while the rest of us go about our business." That was the old world—the siloed world in which churn and retention were the sole problems of the CS organization.

Soon many of you figured out that you couldn't fully address these (and other) issues without integrating all the post-sales functions, including Professional Services, Support, Training (and pretty much everyone else) into an org structure that would drive sustainable growth through customer retention and expansion. Today, some of you are even taking this a step further by bringing in functions such as Sales, Product, Marketing, and Account Management to develop and execute cross-company efforts related to renewals, upsell, advocacy, and even pre-sales. You're bringing the entire organization together and, in some cases, connecting the efforts to your critical external partners. Most of you no longer see Customer Success in terms of firefighting and defense but as a critical way to drive revenue growth. Better yet, many of you now believe that you can monetize CS. You're convincing customers to actually pay for services from which they're getting so much value.

That said, the field of CS is not all unicorns and rainbows. We're living in a very different world from the one that existed just a few years ago. Do any of you have an unlimited budget from your CFO, customers who renew with no problems, customers who are always willing to accept price hikes and buy everything you sell? Most SaaS firms are not enjoying these situations. Instead, times are more challenging. Instead, SaaS companies and their CS organizations have arrived at a crossroads.

Today, some investors are even beginning to doubt the long-term margin potential of SaaS companies[3]—a lack of faith with huge implications for valuations. As you can see in Figure 11.1, SaaS companies—overall—are making progress. But they are not all created equal. And the SaaS industry is far from the 40 to 50 percent terminal operating margins at which many on-premise software companies are currently trading.

The long-term profit potential of every SaaS business is based on four drivers:

- **Total Addressable Market:** The bigger the TAM, the more growth can persist instead of decelerating.
- **Gross Retention:** Companies with a leaky bucket have to spend a ton of money on Sales and Marketing merely to tread water. In the

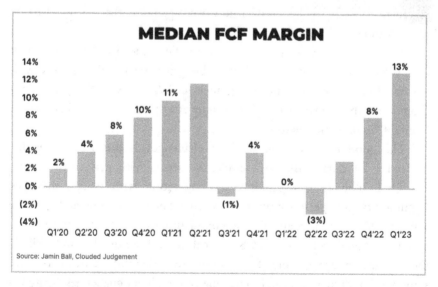

Figure 11.1   Median free cash flow (FCF) margin of SaaS companies from Q1 2020 to Q1 2023.

long term, this game always fails, which is why CS, and especially Digital CS, has never been more important.

- **Gross Margin:** As we've seen over time, 60 percent gross margin companies and 80 percent companies are assigned radically different values.
- **Customer Acquisition Cost:** The best companies figure out ways to bring in revenue (in scalable ways), whether through Product-Led Growth, Channel, or Land + Expand.

The bottom line is this: If you don't have one or two of these levers working for your company at exceptional levels, it will be hard to make the SaaS model work over the long haul. And if you don't reach terminal profitability quickly enough, you *will* be disrupted.

Do More ~~with Less~~ by Reinventing Your Organization

Today, many customers are saying, "I'm a fan of Customer Success, but there are a dozen people reaching out to me from your company every day with different messages. Do your people talk to each other?" Meanwhile, many CFOs and investors are saying, "I like this CS thing, but what can we do *without* having to hire more people?"

In sum, what we hear—over and over again—is that we need to do more with less.

Truth be told, we're not in love with the expression "do more with less." We believe that the key to sustainable growth is not doing more with less but doing more by reinventing ourselves. We believe CS organizations should give themselves permission to reinvent themselves, and that's where Digital CS enters the picture.

The good news, despite all these challenges, is that technology has evolved a lot during the last decade. We see it with generative AI and ChatGPT blowing our minds every day, along with in-app messages, Community, and personalization. Customer Success no longer has to be about CSMs working manually and conducting QBRs. Thanks to new and emerging digital technologies, CS orgs can scale more quickly and easily as their companies grow. Many of you are already doing this. Many of you have some kind of digital motion. In fact, one of the bigger challenges facing CS leaders today is not having too few digital motions but having too many.

Think about your typical customer. They log into your app and see messages that the CS team hasn't been involved in coordinating. You give them seven different websites where they can log in to find training, submit a product request, open a support case, get emails about webinars, listen to the Sales team tell them about a new product—and none of the functions responsible for all this messaging is coordinating with any of the others.

In other words, while digital technology has been evolving, the customer experience (in many instances) has been *devolving*—and it's only going to get worse if we unleash GPT to start spamming our customers.

We need to embrace a different way—and that way is staring us right in the face in the form of our phones. It's something every B2C app has figured out. Because B2C companies don't have CSMs, they've figured out how to guide Nick through his Taylor Swift experience on Spotify without any assistance from a human. They use digital means to tell him about new albums and upcoming concerts.

From Science Fiction to CS Fact

Not so long ago, the notion that tech-powered superintelligence would support our day-to-day lives was the stuff of science fiction. Today we weave in and out of digitally guided journeys and virtual realities just as seamlessly as we navigate real-world experiences. This is becoming increasingly true in the world of Customer Success, where bionic CSMs are now unlocking the power of AI to do more with less.

As the field of CS matures, Digital-led strategies are enabling CS teams to expand their reach, efficiently scale their operations, and deliver more value to customers. Many CS leaders are studying where their teams spend their time and which low-value activities can be eliminated or accelerated via generative AI. Already, some CS organizations are using AI to:

- **Reduce Meeting Prep Time:** CSMs spend a lot of time preparing executives with notes on upcoming client meetings. Such tasks can easily be done by AI.
- **Reduce Support Time:** Although Customer Success does not equal Support, CSMs inevitably spend time fielding technical questions. AI can be used to instantly scan the corpus of knowledge in documentation and support cases, enabling CSMs to answer client questions on the fly.

- **Simplify Knowledge Transfer:** When an account is transitioned (because of turnover, promotions, etc.), the incoming CSM may spend inordinate amounts of time learning the history of the customer. AI can greatly accelerate this learning curve.

As organizations scale their CS operations, it's becoming table stakes to invest in digital-led strategies. But digital tactics require powerful data analytics, automation, and more. That's where AI enters the picture. With AI, CSMs can quickly access insights from rich data into what isn't working and where customer sentiment may be dropping. That way, there are no surprises in customer health, and the CS team gains the power to intervene and course correct wherever needed. AI may not literally give CSMs the power to see the future, but it can enable them to predict how likely renewals are with a simple glance at a health scorecard.

In the very near future, AI will be the hidden weapon in a CS professional's arsenal. It will handle the heavy lifting of analyzing large amounts of data, automating repetitive tasks, and providing real-time insights. It will free up CSMs to focus on relationship-building and high-value engagements of Customer Success.

And as AI continues to improve, becoming easier to manage and configure, you will soon reach a point where you can simply say to it: "Give me a report of all the customers with health scores under 80 who are renewing in 90 days with no recent executive contact." That day is almost here—and it's a day that Gainsight is helping to make possible.

But advances in AI aren't the only things driving the evolution of Digital CS. So are innovations in the field of Customer Education. In fact, we believe the integration of Digital CE solutions with Digital CS, CX, Community, and customer hub platforms will prove to be a watershed in the history of the SaaS industry. The ability of CE to integrate key learning paths and personalized training as part of your customers' end-to-end journey will better enable them to use your products and help you scale your CSMs, driving faster Time to Value. Combine CE tools with a customer hub, and you create a single destination that guides users to the right training at the right time, helps them engage with other community members, and allows them to view personalized on-demand webinars and other content.

CE is currently in a position very similar to that of CS 10 years ago, when there were only a few hundred CSMs worldwide. Now there are a half million because the growth of SaaS demanded a new function to oversee the recurring revenue of subscription businesses. Likewise, the key factor that will drive the explosive growth of CE is the need for SaaS companies to increase profit margins and employ more prudent financial management, which means that bloated CS teams are rapidly becoming a thing of the past.

As business leaders and CS leaders search for ways to tighten cost structures, many will land on Customer Education as a solution. Why? Because it's a business process that can transcend the entire customer journey, generating a positive and actionable impact on the customer—from the moment they begin evaluating a vendor all the way through renewal, expansion, and advocacy.

We believe CE is leading us to a prized goal of the CSM profession—toward a day when CSMs don't have to spend time on essential, but routine, functions but can dedicate more time to unleashing their individual creativity to drive revenue growth.

Digital Enables a More Human Experience

B2C firms use digital to provide a very human experience, which is why many of you are already digitizing your customer experience in some way. Digital CS helps your CSMs shift the focus from repetitive and often tedious tasks to higher-value activities.

No more one-on-one training for new customers. No more one-on-one demos for customers to show them a new feature. No more manually drafted emails with release notes. Digital CS gives your CSMs more time to connect with customers. More time to build relationships. More time to understand the outcomes and experiences that every customer wants to have. And by the way, Digital CS will go a long way toward alleviating CSM burnout.

On the other side, your customers will absolutely love Digital CS. They'll love it because we're moving away from the antiquated notion that small customers should receive only digital self-service while big customers get a high-touch experience. That view is not only old-fashioned but misguided.

We'll tell you a secret: Some of your biggest customers don't want to do another QBR. We know that sounds a bit controversial, but many of your largest clients would absolutely love more digital experiences, talking with you only when necessary. And some of your small customers would really love a high-touch experience.

Your investors and CFOs will also love Digital CS. Just imagine these people nodding and smiling as they relish the thought of higher NRR at a lower cost. What's not to love?

Ten years ago, we introduced this supernerdy equation. Some of you probably remember it: $CS = CO + CX$. Customer success is getting your customers to the outcomes they're seeking with a great experience. That equation is still true today, but we can change it. We can make it even better by adding digital. Digital is going to turbocharge your teams. By taking Customer Success to the power of digital, you're going to be able to deliver a totally different experience for your customers. Digital will make you more effective in front of your customers, during QBRs, and via emails. Digital will also deliver a better experience for your customers, whether it's on the customer hub, in your product, or anywhere else.

The early days of Customer Success were very artisanal. They were about figuring things out as we went along. Digital technology will allow us to become better artisans. It will enable us to accomplish all the things that we, as humans, excel at accomplishing while relegating the less pleasant, low-value activities to computers.

That's the promise and the reality of Digital Customer Success. It's giving us the freedom to be more human.

Acknowledgments

Like every SaaS solution ever made, *Digital Customer Success* is the product of multiple minds. It's the fruit of a collaboration between many different individuals, teams, and companies—dedicated professionals who devoted thousands of hours to developing, testing, iterating, and sharing the Digital CS strategies, tactics, use cases, initiatives, and learnings that you'll find in this book. We are grateful and delighted by the magnitude of their accomplishment.

Special thanks to Melissa Allen, Senior Manager, CS Operations at Okta and Kari Ardalan, Global Head of Digital and Scale Success at Qualtrics for taking time from their beyond-busy schedules to talk with us about their pioneering digital initiatives.

Special thanks, also, to the other Gainsight customers who allowed us to share their stories, insights, and recommendations. They include executives from Alteryx, Dealerware, Docebo, Drift, Gitlab, Gong, Popmenu, Shiji ReviewPro, Samsara, and Unqork.

Just as important were the many—and massive—contributions made by Gainsight's leaders and their teams. This book would not have been possible without the contributions of Gainsters, past and present, including:

- Karl Rumelhart
- Tyler McNally
- Joris Dieben
- Harshita Banka
- Matthew Wasley

- Seth Wylie
- Lane Holt
- Tori Jeffcoat
- Aarthi Rayapura

This book is their achievement, as much as ours.

Finally, we'd like to thank Gainsight's content and design team, as well as freelance writer Peter Gerardo for helping to transmute large quantities of research data and interviews into a polished manuscript. Their organizational and developmental editing talents were instrumental to the creation of the final manuscript.

About the Authors

Nick Mehta, CEO, Gainsight

Nick Mehta (he/him) is the CEO of Gainsight, the platform that helps companies of all sizes and industries drive durable growth through customer-led and product-led strategies.

Gainsight is a five-time *Forbes* Cloud 100 recipient, placing #1 on Glassdoor's Best Places to Work list for 2023, and Nick has been named one of the Top SaaS CEOs by the *Software Report* four times and Entrepreneur of the Year for Northern California by EY in 2020.

He is a member of the Board of Directors at F5 (NASDAQ:FFIV) and PubMatic Inc. (NASDAQ: PUBM) and has coauthored three books—- *Customer Success*, *The Customer Success Economy*, and *Customer Communities*. He is passionate about family, football, philosophy, physics, fashion, SaaS, parody music videos, The Boss, and everything Taylor Swift. People told him it's impossible to combine all of those interests, but Nick has made it his life's mission to try.

Kellie Capote, CCO, Gainsight

Kellie Capote is the Chief Customer Officer at Gainsight. Kellie has spent the last five years involved in building and leading the success organization at Gainsight. In her current role as CCO, she leads the post-sales organization that includes the CSM, Support, Professional Services, and CS Ops & Scale orgs. She is deeply focused on driving positive business outcomes for

Gainsight's customers along with exceptional customer experience. She has a passion for the mission-critical role that CS plays within organizations as a growth engine for their business and is dedicated to helping define this vision and strategy for others.

Prior to Gainsight, Kellie spent her career in customer-facing roles spanning across Sales, Account Management, and Customer Success, with a background in HCM. She has found her forever home in Customer Success at the intersection of what she is energized by most: forging prosperous customer relationships and professional growth for teammates.

Kellie and her husband live in Austin, Texas, with their two daughters.

Notes

Chapter 1

1. Nick Mehta and Allison Pickens, *The Customer Success Economy: Why Every Aspect of Your Business Model Needs a Paradigm Shift* (Hoboken, NJ: John Wiley & Sons, 2020).
2. Gainsight, Inc., "The Customer Success Index, 2022" (March 2022). https://info.gainsight.com/the-customer-success-index-2022_ebook .html.
3. Gartner, "Market Guide for Customer Success Management Platforms", Michael Maziarka, Maria Marino, Robert Blaisdell, John Quaglietta, Jennifer MacIntosh, 30 August 2023. GARTNER is a registered trademark of Gartner, Inc. and/or its affiliates and is used herein with permission. All rights reserved.
4. Keitt, T. J., "Build the Case for a Customer Success Management Program Now." Forrester.com blogs, September 14, 2020.
5. Bain & Company, "CS Outlook—Initial Insights," February 2023. Bain Company, Inc. is not affiliated with Gainsight and the information contained in this book has not been reviewed or endorsed by Bain & Company.
6. Excerpted from "Introducing customer success 2.0: The new growth engine", January 2018, McKinsey & Company, www.mckinsey.com. Copyright (c) 2023 McKinsey & Company. All rights reserved. Reprinted by permission.

Chapter 2

1. "Why Were Tech Stocks Down in 2022—And How Long Will the Slump Last?" *Forbes*, January 19, 2023. https://www.forbes.com/sites/qai/2023/01/19/why-were-tech-stocks-down-in-2022-and-how-long-will-the-slump-last/?sh=5bf486767f16.
2. Keerthi Vedantam, "Tech Layoffs: U.S. Companies that Have Cut Jobs in 2022 and 2023," *Crunchbase News*, March 3, 2023. https://news.crunchbase.com/startups/tech-layoffs/.
3. Melissa Allen, interview by Peter Gerardo, July 28, 2023.
4. Jeff Beaumont, "Digital and Scale Are Not Just for the Longtail," presentation, Pulse Conference, San Francisco, CA, August 2022.
5. Gainsight, Inc., "Case Study: ReviewPro," 2022. https://info.gainsight.com/cs-reviewpro-casestudy.html.
6. Daniel McCarthy, "HelloFresh Has a Bigger Customer Retention Problem than Blue Apron," LinkedIn, October 24, 2017. https://www.linkedin.com/pulse/hellofresh-has-bigger-customer-retention-problem-than-daniel-mccarthy/.
7. Excerpted from "Introducing customer success 2.0: The new growth engine", January 2018, McKinsey & Company, www.mckinsey.com. Copyright (c) 2023 McKinsey & Company. All rights reserved. Reprinted by permission.

Chapter 3

1. Zendesk, "Zendesk Customer Experience Trends Report 2024." https://cxtrends.zendesk.com.
2. Gartner, Gartner Says Only 9% of Customers Report Solving Their Issues Completely via Self-Service, 25 September 2019 [https://www.gartner.com/en/newsroom/press-releases/2019-09-25-gartner-says-only-9--of-customers-report-solving-thei]. This Gartner content is archived and is included for historical context only.
3. Rocketlane, "The State of Customer Onboarding 2024." https://www.rocketlane.com/state-of-onboarding.
4. Steve Cornwell, interview by Peter Gerardo, August 16, 2023.
5. Gainsight, Inc., "How Gong Uses Community to Fuel ARR and Customer Retention," 2022. https://www.gainsight.com/customers/how-gong-uses-community-to-fuel-arr-and-customer-retention/.

Chapter 4

1. Gainsight, Inc., "How Gong Uses Community to Fuel ARR and Customer Retention," 2022. https://www.gainsight.com/customers/how-gong-uses-community-to-fuel-arr-and-customer-retention/.
2. Gainsight, Inc., "Case Study: How Docebo Community Hit 96% P2P Support in Less than a Year," December 6, 2022. https://www.insided.com/blog/case-study-how-docebo-hits-96-percent-peer-to-peer-support/.
3. Gainsight, Inc., "Case Study: Dealerware Uses Gainsight CS + PX to Scale Without Increasing Headcount," 2022. https://info.gainsight.com/cs-dealerware-case-study.html.
4. Gainsight, Inc., "TigerText Increases Efficiency by 8.25% Using Gainsight CoPilot to Save 3.3 Hours per CSM per Week," 2016.
5. Gainsight, Inc., "RiskIQ Achieves Net Retention over 100% by Scaling Customer Success and Operational Excellence with Gainsight." https://info.gainsight.com/riskiq-case-study.html.
6. Melissa Allen, interview by Peter Gerardo, July 28, 2023.

Chapter 5

1. Excerpted from "Finding the right digital balance in B2B customer experience", April 2017, McKinsey & Company, www.mckinsey.com Copyright (c) 2023 McKinsey & Company. All rights reserved. Reprinted by permission.
2. Danny Pancratz, interview by Becky May, May 18, 2023.
3. Gainsight, Inc., "Alteryx Customer Success Finds Digital Scale and Efficiency," https://www.gainsight.com/customers/alteryx-customer-success-finds-digital-scale-and-efficiency.

Chapter 6

1. Jim Jefferies, "High & Dry" clip, https://www.facebook.com/watch/?v=921112639308564.
2. Case Study: ReviewPro (San Francisco: Gainsight, Inc., 2022).
3. Justin Smith, interviewed by Peter Gerardo, August 14, 2023.
4. Scott Ernest and Bart Hammond, Opening Keynote Address, Pulse Conference, San Francisco, CA, May 17, 2023.

Chapter 7

1. Bain & Company, "Retaining Customers Is the Real Challenge," January 20, 2006. https://www.bain.com/insights/retaining-customers-is-the-real-challenge/.
2. Gainsight, Inc., "SaaS Market Report 2022," 2022. https://info.gainsight.com/saas-market-report-resource-whitepaper.html.
3. Gainsight, Inc., "Dealerware Uses Gainsight CS + PX to Scale Without Increasing Headcount." https://info.gainsight.com/cs-dealerware-case-study.html.
4. Kari Ardalan, interview by Peter Gerardo, June 23, 2023.
5. Benjamin Weister, "Here's What Happens When Your Lawyer Uses ChatGPT," *New York Times*, May 27, 2023. https://www.nytimes.com/2023/05/27/nyregion/avianca-airline-lawsuit-chatgpt.html.

Chapter 8

1. Melissa Allen, interview by Peter Gerardo, July 28, 2023.
2. Jess Kitt, "Improving Internal Efficiency with Intentional Automation," presentation, Pulse Conference, San Francisco, CA, May 17, 2023.

Chapter 9

1. Kari Ardalan, interview by Peter Gerardo, June 23, 2023.
2. Nick Mehta, Dan Steinman, and Lincoln Murphy, *Customer Success: How Innovative Companies Are Reducing Churn and Growing Recurring Revenue* (Hoboken, NJ: John Wiley & Sons, 2016).
3. Gainsight, Inc., "Dealerware Uses Gainsight CS + PX to Scale Without Increasing Headcount." https://info.gainsight.com/cs-dealerware-case-study.html.

Chapter 11

1. Nick Mehta, Dan Steinman, and Lincoln Murphy, *Customer Success: How Innovative Companies Are Reducing Churn and Growing Recurring Revenue* (Hoboken, NJ: John Wiley & Sons, 2016).
2. Chip Heath and Dan Heath, *The Power of Moments: Why Certain Experiences Have Extraordinary Impact* (New York: Simon & Schuster, 2017).
3. Jamin Ball, "Clouded Judgement 7.21.23—Are Software Companies Bad Business," https://cloudedjudgement.substack.com/p/clouded-judgement-72123-are-software.

Index

A

Account executive/managers
    (persona), 118
Adoption, 23
  journey, customer
      perception, 108–109
  phase, 149, 187
Advanced analytics, leveraging, 151
Allen, Melissa, 24, 66–67, 141
Alteryx, communications
    personalization, 80, 81f, 82
Analytics, usage, 30
Annual recurring revenue
    (ARR), 61
  growth, 20
Ardalan, Kari, 121, 122, 157–159,
    163–164, 167, 173
Artificial intelligence (AI)
  AI-driven risk management,
    112–115
  AI-powered sponsor-tracking
    feature (Gainsight), 114f
  role, 120–126

At-risk accounts, rescue, 8
At-risk customers, 163
  consideration, 186
Audience, understanding,
    179–180
Automated advocacy programs,
    97, 100–103
Automated CS journey playbook,
    example, 188f
Automated email messaging,
    usage, 186–187
Automated emails, sending, 190
Automation
  scaling, 67
  usage, 147–150
Avianca, lawsuit, 123

B

Ballhaussen, Adam, 58
Bandwidth, extension/
    examination, 139–140
Bionic CSMs, 37–39, 201
Business owners, meeting, 159

Business-to-business (B2B)
cloud computing, 94
consumers preferences, 11
customer demands, 3
customer expectations, 151
customer alienation (problem), 75
solution, 186–187
Business-to-consumer (B2C)
ecommerce retailers,
transactions, 3
environment, user
expectations, 36
solution, 186–187
ButcherBox subscription, 171

C
ChatGPT, 123
Churn busters, 6–8
Click-through rates,
improvement, 164
Closed-loop feedback
programs, 94–99
Closed-loop programs, rollout, 100
Collaboration, elements, 160–165
Collaborative success hub,
creation, 66
Communications
channel selection, 136–139,
189, 191
uniformity (ensuring), 150–151
Community
action plan, learnings
(compilation), 184
cohorts, strategy, 62
expertise, usage, 74
hub, 169, 177–186
experience, 77

job postings, relationship, 47
purposes, determination, 183
Q&A/discussion, impact, 56
strategy, 179, 180, 182
learnings, compilation, 184
support-focused Community, 180
Third Place role, 47–48
use cases, goals/priorities
determination
(relationship), 177–179
visitors, attraction, 180–181
Company-wide digital program
governance, 155
Connection, impact, 77–78
Continuous improvement, 148
Cornwell, Steve, 44
Cross-company efforts,
development/execution, 198
Cross-functional alignment
collaboration, 155
growth, 158
management, 77
results, sharing, 168–169
teams, communication/
governance, 160–161
CTA playbook, usage, 150
Customer Acquisition Cost
(CAC), 32, 200
reduction, 24, 25
Customer Education, 42
impact, 43
Customer Experience, 16
digital CE, digital
CS (integration), 42–45
disjointed CX
cause, 157
production, 179

improvement, 25–26
Customer-facing teams, 73
Customer Outcomes (CO), 16
Customers
  adoption journey,
      perception, 108–109
  at-risk customers,
      consideration, 186
  base, cultivation, 25
  conversations, basis, 54
  data, vendor mining, 10
  G2 reviews, 168
  high-touch experience, 203
  hub, 169, 177–186
    resource, 54, 56, 76
  importance, 32–33
  interaction, 150–151
  journey, data (sharing), 170–171
  life cycle stage, messaging
      campaigns (design), 187
  loyalty (building), digital CS
      (impact), 197–200
  onboarding, company usage, 37
  one-to-many customer
      communications, 78–80, 80f
  renewal rate, elevation, 68
  retention, improvement, 40
  segments, basis, 49f
  selection, 135–136
  spamming (avoidance), throttle
      (usage), 190–191
  success, 39
Customer Satisfaction (CSAT)
  Onboarding CSAT survey, 89
  question, 48
  scores, 29, 99
Customer Success (CS)

automated CS journey
    playbook, example, 188f
  building, 17
  company-wide imperative, 8–9
  content, accessibility, 75
  customers, importance, 26–28
  definition (Gainsight), 6
    durable growth engine, 21–29
  efficiency, 55f
  efforts, insights, 10
  fact/fiction, separation, 201–203
  focus, questions, 7
  future, appearance, 44
  growth, product (impact), 28–29
  high-speed evolution, 1
  human/digital dilemma, 2–4
  invention, 4–6
  journey, 27
    automation, 187–194
  laws (Gainsight), 17
  maturation, 7
  metrics-driven strategies, 17
  model, usage, 106
  monetization, 9
  net revenue-generator, 8–9
  offense, 28
  operations, investment, 17
  organizations
    budget pressure, increase, 8
    resolution, struggle, 3
  program (launch), digital CS
      (usage), 45–46
  reinvention, timing, 13–17
  teams, building, 20
  technology/data, usage,
      169–170
  work, human element, 148

Customer Success Economy, The
      (Mehta), 5
Customer Success
      Management (CSM)
   bionic CSMs, 37–39, 201
   calendar, addition, 149
   CSM-to-Account ratio,
      increase, 82
   CTA playbook, usage, 150
   importance, 7
   manager, persona, 79, 85
   occupational hazards, 86
   persona, 112, 118
   pooled CSM teams,
      creation, 12
   post content, 181
   results, aggregation, 168–169
   virtual CSM, creation, 12
Customer Success Platform
      (CSP), leveraging, 22
Customer Success Qualified Leads
      (CSQLs), 28
Customization, scaling, 67

D
Data
   clarity, 134
   leverage, 191
   sharing, 170–171
Dealerware, 60–61
Dedicated leader, appointment,
      165–167
Defensive strategies, shift, 10
Deployment, 22
Deployment, Engagement,
      Adoption, and ROI (DEAR)
      Framework, 22–23

Detractor
   concerns (acknowledgment),
      Gainsight email
      (usage), 98f
   management, flowchart
      (Gainsight), 97f
Digital Customer Education
   digital CS, integration, 42–45
   platforms, adoption, 43
Digital communications,
      checkpoints
      (establishment), 187
Digital Customer Success
      (digital CS)
   approach, 55f
   benefits, 98
   community, impact, 77–78
   concept, 4
   definition, 39–42
   digital CE, digital
      CS (integration), 42–45
   growth, 41
   impact, 197–200
   maturity
      linear progression, 57f
      model, 53
      three Ps, 56f
   models, 14f, 15f
      improvement, 49f
   org chart, example, 146f
   personalized stage/phase,
      54, 56f, 59–62, 93
   phases, 94
   predictive stage/phase, 54, 56f,
      62, 64, 111
   proactive stage/phase, 54, 56,
      56f, 58–59

program
creation, 170
launch, 46
org design types, 145f
proactive stage, launch, 71
team, collaboration, 158–160
scaling, 24–25
strategic program, 35
strategy, achievements, 39, 51
success, three Ps, 54
team, meeting, 97
testing, 49–50
usage, 45–46
Digital-first approach, 4
Digital-first journey, 12
Digital initiative, launch, 129
Digital journey, 66
Digital-led experience, human-led
experience (mixture), 49f
Digital-led onboarding, 84–87
best practices, 87–90
program, absence (impact),
86–87
Digital-led strategies, impact, 201
Digital maturity, journey
(Okta), 66–68
Digital Maturity Spectrum, 94,
111, 140, 170
Digital process, incorporation, 25
Digital program rollout,
testing/learning (three-phase
approach), 135–136
Digital technology, usage, 3
Digital toolkit, optimization, 175
Disjointed CX
cause, 157
production, 179

Docebo, solutions, 58
Drift
impact, 105–107
value, 107
Driving prospects,
consideration, 186
Durable business
growth, 9
engine, 21–29
playbook, 21
strategies, usage, 19

E
EBR, coordination, 149
Economic climate change,
impact, 38
Ecosystem
Community positioning, 183
examination, 183–184
Education leader (persona), 95, 104
Education services leader
(persona), 73, 85
Efficiency
driving, community/customer
hub (usage), 17
improvement, automation
(usage), 147–150
increase, digital CS (impact), 39
Emails
automation, 169
campaigns, impact, 59
programs, usage, 66
task, automation, 12
viewing, 194
welcome email, example, 63f
Embedded knowledge center,
impact, 59

End-to-end workflows, 23
Engagement, 22
Ernest, Scott, 106, 107
Executive buy-in,
        obtaining, 167–168
Expansion opportunities,
        increase, 40
Expansion rates, impact, 164
Expansion selling,
        optimization, 117–120

F
Feature-discovery algorithms,
        usage, 10
Federated search and
        integration, usage, 56
Feedback
    receiving/impact, 96–97
Floqast, automated advocacy
        program, 102–103
Full-Time Equivalent (FTE)
        savings, examination, 167
Functionality, 30–31

G
Gainsight
    AI-powered sponsor-tracking
        feature, 114f
    customers, alert (usage), 59–60
    data, input, 67
    data points, integration, 66
    detractor management,
        flowchart, 97f
    email, sample, 98f
    engagement platform,
        164–165
    in-app survey, 118f

    initiatives, 143
    Knowledge Center bot,
        usage, 191–192
    onboarding checklist,
        example, 144f
    pooled CSM model
        adoption, 42
    product
        analytics, 164–165
        usage, 81
    purpose statement, 2
    Sales User Win-Back, 107
    Text Analytics, usage, 99
    welcome email, exam-
        ples, 63f, 131f
Gamification, usage, 74
Goals, determination, 177–179
Gong, stage transition, 56, 58
Go-to-Market (GTM)
    implications, 161
    team, collaboration, 32
Gross margin, 200
Gross retention, 199–200
Gross revenue retention (GRR)
    improvement, 39
    increase, 6
Growth Index (Edison Partners), 20

H
Hammond, Bart, 106, 107
Health scores, influence, 101
Heath, Chip/Dan, 198
High-value activities, CSMs
        (usage), 147
Human connections,
        development, 185–186

Human Customer Success
    Management, accessibility, 75
Human experience (enabling),
    digital CS (usage),
    203–204
Human-First approach/
    strategies, 2, 4, 29
  digital-first strategies, blend, 13
  maintenance, 17
Human interactions, user
    preference, 326
Human-led motions, digital-led
    motions (combination), 15f
Humanness, ability (increase), 197
Human voices, amplification, 189

I
Impact, measurement,
    132–134
In-app
  bots, usage, 41
  communications, 169, 194
  content, 79, 189
  recommendation, usage, 64
  guides, 191
  knowledge bot, usage, 56, 68
  messages, 189, 190
  targeting, usage, 60
  usage, 192–193
    messaging, usage, 38, 66,
      186–187, 188f, 194
    product communication,
      usage, 59
    survey (Gainsight), 118f
    tutorials, usage, 168
    viewing, 194
Inboxes, usage, 80–84

In-dashboard pop-ups,
    usage, 89
Industry analysis, basis, 54
In-product experiences/
    messaging, ownership
    determination, 162
Integrated customer journey,
    creation, 17
Intelligent Journey
    Orchestration, usage, 64
Internal use cases, AI (usage), 122
Investor success, 39

J
James, Neil, 27
  Job postings, 47
Joint projects, number
    (limitations), 161
Journey Orchestrator, 106
    strategy, implementation, 64

K
Key performance indicators (KPIs)
    approach, 183
    setup, 26
Key workflow interruption
    (avoidance), in-app
    messages (usage), 192–193
Kitt, Jess, 147, 149
Knowledge Base, 75
    online community,
      combination, 75
Knowledge Center bot, 46, 60–61
    impact, 61
    usage, 191–192
Knowledge transfer,
    simplification, 202

L

Lagging indicator, selection, 133

Leading indicator
lagging indicator, correlation, 164
selection, 133

Learnings, compilation, 184

Life cycle
moment
consideration, 189
selection, 130–132, 141
stage, 151
messaging campaigns,
design, 187

Livestream events, 167

Long-term success (fueling),
durable business strategies
(usage), 19

M

Machine-learning techniques,
usage, 10

Margins, company improvement, 41

Marketing leader (persona), 101

Martinez v. Delta Air Lines, 123

Maturity levels, occupying,
64–65

MAU/MAC, reach
(comparison), 163

Median free cash flow (FCF)
margin, 199f

Meeting prep time, reduction, 201

Messaging
campaigns, design, 187
quality, importance, 151
targeting, basis, 189–190

Metrics-based business, 10–11

Milestone, selection, 133–134

Momentum, 140–141

Multichannel analytics, usage, 64

N

Net Promoter Scores (NPS),
29, 43, 61, 120, 164
Admin NPS, renewal
(correlation), 132
award, 102
feedback, 106
in-app end user survey, 168–169
increase, 99
question, usage, 96
responses rate, increase, 95
surveys, usage, 90, 102, 137
usage, 29

Net revenue-generator, 8–9

Net revenue retention
(NRR), 64, 200
achievement, 21
improvement, 39
increase, 6, 87
understanding, 17

North Stars
focus, 31
selection, 26

NVRs, storage, 66

O

Objective, Goals, Measures,
and Strategies (OGSM)
framework, 184

Objectives and Key Results
(OKR) framework,
usefulness, 184

Okta, 24
branding, emails (alignment), 67

data points, 141
digital maturity journey, 66–68
Onboarding checklist (Gainsight),
    example, 144f
Onboarding CSAT survey, 89
Onboarding programs, 87–88
Onboarding stage, 187
One-to-many
    campaigns, 143
        communications program, 84
        target audience dependence,
            81, 83
    customer communications,
        78–80, 80f
        admin survey, 99
        revision, 161
    emails, 37
        obtaining, 14
    "Fitness Success" (Peloton), 12
    programs, usage, 59
Ongoing education, 90
Online knowledge base,
    providing, 74
Operational efficiency,
    customer education
    (impact), 43–44
Optimized expansion selling,
    117–120
    Organization, reinvention,
        200–201
Org design, types, 145f

P
P2P resources, 73
Pancratz, Danny, 76, 77
Peer-to-peer (P2P) response
    rate, increase, 58

Peloton
    paradigm, 11–13
    strategies, combination, 12
    users, categories, 11
Perfection, problem, 68–69
Personalization, impact, 80
Personalized customer
    experience, 3–4
Personas
    consideration, 189
    importance, 73, 79
    selection, 135–136
    targeting, 187
    understanding, 179–180
Plant, Anthony, 108
Platform resources, bookmarks,
    76
Pooled Customer Success
    Management (pooled
    CSM), 40
    model, usage, 59
    teams, creation, 12
Pooled Customer Success team,
    personalized email address
    (usage), 80
Popmenu (efficiency
    improvement), automation
    (usage), 147–150
Post-sales communications, single
    owner establishment, 157
Power of Moments, The (Heath/
    Heath), 198
Prescriptive adoption journeys,
    103–105
Priorities, determination,
    177–179
Problem, solutions, 99–100

Product
  adoption
    campaigns, 90
    improvement, 40
  impact, 28–29
  leader (persona), 95, 104, 112, 116
  level, 151
  manager (persona), 73, 79, 85, 95,
        104, 112, 116
  outcome-related features, 30
  roadmap, 160
    building, 25–26
    rethinking, 30–31
  team, meeting, 97
  user interaction, knowledge
        center bot (usage), 191–192
Product-idea-and-update
        use case, 177
Product-Led Growth (PLG), 78
Product Management & Marketing
        (PMM), 158
Product Marketing Manager
        (PMM), 166
Programmatic value realiza-
        tion, 115–117
Purpose (defining), digital process
        (incorporation), 25

Q
Qualtrics
  CS/Support, role, 122
  process, 159–160
  reach, extension, 164
  scoreboard/track, 165f
  team, metric, 167
Quarterly Business Reviews
        (QBRs), 38, 204

  conducting, 200
  decks (task), automation, 12
  engagement, avoidance, 41
  storage, 66

R
Reach (metric), 133
  MAU/MAC, comparison, 163
Recurring revenue,
        surprises (avoidance),
        21–23
Redwine, Morgan, 61, 164
Reference database,
        maintenance, 101
Relationship (building), inboxes
        (usage), 80–84
Reporting (task), automation, 12
Retained revenue rate, 21
Retention rates, impact, 164
Return on investment
        (ROI), 22–23, 85
  achievement, 23
  driving, 61
  increase, 87
  model, production, 183
Revenue
  boosters, 6–8
  impact, customer education
        (impact), 44
  maintenance, 158
Risk-averse organization, 182
RiskIQ, 64
Role-based landing page,
        impact, 59
Rumelhart, Karl, 122
Runaway accretion,
        approach, 140–142

S

Salesforce
  data, input, 67
  data points, integration, 66
Sales-only focus, 6
Sales User Win-Back (Gainsight),
    107
Samsara
  digital-led onboarding, best
      practices, 87–90
  ongoing education/
      engagement, 90
  welcome email, 89
Save-the-date promotions, 167
Scale, preparation, 142–144, 147
Scale (increase), digital CS
    (impact), 39
Scaled team, 158
Scaling, quest, 36–37
Scope creep, examination,
    134–135
Segment, 151
Self-service
  customer interest, 54
  enablement, 72–73
  improvement, 74–75
  information, access, 27
  options, 40
  portals, examination, 163–164
  users, empowerment, 72
  user preference, 36
Self-serving communications,
    avoidance, 193
Shared cross-functional
    framework, 161–162
Shared project milestones, 161–162
Shiji ReviewPro, 27

Single digital destination, usage, 64
SMB
  clients/customers, 38, 40, 51
  segment, 48
Smith, Justin, 102–103
Software, customer consumption
    (shift), 38
Software as a Service (SaaS)
  B2B SaaS space, 177
  businesses
    focus, 186
    potential, 199
  growth, 203
  industry, changes, 19
  leaders, customer education
      misconception, 44–45
  organizations, capability, 171
  sales-driven SaaS model, 156–157
Software as a Service
    (SaaS) companies
  automated/human-led CS
      paradigm trap, 9–11
  gamification, usage, 74
  median free cash flow (FCF)
      margin, 199f
  potential, 199
  resolution, struggle, 3
Spending, CFO reduction, 20
Spotify, usage, 15, 201
Starbucks, Third Place, 47
SteerCo job, 159
Stickiness, focus, 30–31
Strategy/approvals, ownership
    determination, 162–163
Subject Matter Expert (SME),
    42, 177, 182
  team, impact, 161

Subscription model, 8
Support-focused Community, 180
Support Manager, persona, 79, 85
Support representative,
    accessibility, 75
Support time, reduction, 201

T
Target audience, channels
    (selection), 137–139
Targeted engagements, 61
Teammate success, 39
Technology, evolution, 38
Tech Touch, 37–39
    revision, 48, 49f
Telemetry data, importance, 23
Text Analytics (Gainsight),
    usage, 99
Thought leadership site, 157
Throttle, usage, 190–191
Ticket
    deflection, support, 73
    interactivity, 167
TigerConnect, 61
Time to Value (TTV)
    acceleration, 72, 78, 84–85
    decrease, 90
    driving, 202
    improvement, 85
        embedded knowledge center,
            impact, 59
    minimization, 193
Tools, proliferation, 37
Total Addressable Market
    (TAM), 199

Tracking/instrumentation,
    ownership
        determination, 162
Transparency, establishment, 25

U
Unqork
    customer hub power, 76–78
    video series, launch, 77
User
    behavior, influence, 31
    cases, consideration, 178f
    persona/life cycle moment,
        consideration, 189
User Experience (UX)
    focus, 122
    improvement, 40
User Interface (UI), focus, 122

V
Value
    achievement, 23
    customers
        approach, 62, 64
        guidance, Drift
            (impact), 105–107
    examination, organization
        approach, 182–183
    improvement, 36–37
    maximization, 62
    proof, 182
*Varghese v. China Southern
    Airlines,* 123
Variables, vendor scan, 10
Vendors, challenge, 148

Video messaging, usage, 68
Virtual CSM, creation, 12

W
Welcome email (Gainsight),
  examples, 63f, 131f

X
XMI, 157

Z
*Zicherman v. Korean Air
  Lines,* 123